BE AFRAID
BE VERY AFRAID

Other books by Jan Harold Brunvand

Encyclopedia of Urban Legends
Too Good to Be True
The Truth Never Stands in the Way of a Good Story
American Folklore: An Encyclopedia
The Baby Train
Curses! Broiled Again!
The Mexican Pet
The Choking Doberman
The Vanishing Hitchhiker
The Study of American Folklore
Readings in American Folklore

BE AFRAID
BE VERY AFRAID

The Book of Scary
Urban Legends

JAN HAROLD
BRUNVAND

W. W. Norton & Company   New York · London

For information about permission to reproduce selections from this book, write to
Permissions, W. W. Norton & Company, Inc., 500 Fifth Avenue, New York, NY 10110

Lines from the song "Interchange Two Phases" in Chapter 6 are quoted, with permission, from Norman Walker's 2002 CD *Time Tested Tales, Tall and True*, Prairie Pagan Music #01, Regina, SK, Canada. From *While Rome Burns* by Alexander Woollcott, copyright © 1943 by Alexander Woollcott, renewed © 1962 by Joseph P. Hennessey. Used by permission of Viking Penguin, a division of Penguin Group (USA) Inc. Excerpts from "The Current Crop of Ghost Stories" from *Famous Ghost Stories* by Bennett Cerf. Copyright © 1944 by Bennett Cerf. Used by permission of Random House, Inc. "Blind Girls" from *Black Tickets* by Jayne Anne Phillips, copyright © 1979 by Jayne Anne Phillips. Used by permission of the author. "The White Dress" from *The Scary Story Reader* by Richard and Judy Dockery Young. Copyright © 1993. Published by August House Publishers, Inc., and reprinted by permission of Marian Reiner on behalf of the publishers. "Sleepless Nights in Canada" from Ann Landers column, originally published July 30, 1987. Used by permission of Esther P. Lederer and Creators Syndicate, Inc. Reprinted by permission of the publisher from *Land of the Millrats* by Richard M. Dorson, p. 228, Cambridge, Mass.: Harvard University Press, Copyright © 1981 by the President and Fellows of Harvard College. "Never Love a Stranger" by Lynn Darling, copyright © Lynn Darling. Reprinted by permission of Sterling Lord Literistic, Inc.

Manufacturing by Quad/Graphics, Fairfield
Book design by Anna Oler
Production manager: Amanda Morrison

Library of Congress Cataloging-in-Publication Data
Be afraid, be very afraid : the book of scary urban legends / [collected by] Jan Harold Brunvand.— 1st ed.
    p. cm.
  Includes bibliographical references.
  ISBN 978-0-393-32613-0 (pbk.)
1. Urban folklore—United States. 2. Legends—United States. I. Brunvand, Jan Harold.
  GR105.B38 2004
  398.2'0973'091732—dc22   2004011798

W. W. Norton & Company, Inc.
500 Fifth Avenue, New York, N.Y. 10110
www.wwnorton.com

W. W. Norton & Company Ltd.
Castle House, 75/76 Wells Street, London W1t 3QT

7 8 9 0

CONTENTS

A NOTE ON THE TEXTS

The stories in this book that are credited to individuals came from readers of my previous urban legend collections (1981 to 1999) or of my syndicated newspaper columns (1987 to 1992). Some of these people may have changed their names, residences, or occupations since writing to me, but I give the information that was submitted with their stories.

I have not altered the texts except to correct obvious typos and errors of fact. In both the stories from readers and those quoted from published sources, I have occasionally reparagraphed the texts and in the case of stories from readers, slightly changed punctuation and spelling for the sake of consistency. Texts that came to me as e-mail, however, are quoted verbatim—errors, creative punctuation, and all—except as otherwise indicated for the specific reasons stated.

INTRODUCTION

Gore Galore on the
Bedroom Floor

What do you think is scary? A Halloween spook house? A haunted corn maze? A slasher movie? Certainly these kinds of things can give you a shiver, but—really—don't we all know they are just make-believe, acknowledged fictions? In real life, what is more likely to be really scary are things like finding your keys locked in the car, or discovering termites in the foundation of your home, or hearing the telephone ringing in the middle of the night.

Urban legends (ULs) are scary when they combine horror fiction with the details of real life. In typical ULs you encounter shocks such as lurking criminals, threatening maniacs, vague unknown dangers, faulty products, and isolated victims, all set in the context of everyday life. Such stories are told by a friend as something that happened to his or her close acquaintance (a friend of a friend, or a FOAF). Urban legends are packed with local details and related with an air of conviction. While these stories are not literally true, any more than a horror film is, when hearing them we realize that they *could* be true!

Not all urban legends are horrific, and not all horror stories are urban legends, but IMHO (in my humble opinion), as people write in e-mail shorthand, the scariest modern stories are the urban-legendary ones—horror ULs. That's because these scary, creepy, shivery tales always hit close to home, both because of their familiar subject matter and because of the neighborly narrators we hear them from. For example, here's what "Sara," a woman from somewhere in cyberspace, e-mailed me recently after reading one of my urban legend books. She reported that this story, told by her mother, still scares the daylights out of her:

> I heard this story around 1986 from my mother. I was six years old, and to this day I won't stick my hand under the bed at night! I'm not sure where she heard it, though I imagine it was some time in the '60's or '70's in Texas.
>
> This couple is going to visit friends in the next town overnight, and they want to hire a babysitter for their daughter. But she begs and pleads for them to let her stay home alone, and they finally decide okay, she's old enough, they'll leave her without a babysitter for the first time. She's actually a bit nervous about this, but she has a pretty big dog, and she figures he'll protect her if anything happens.
>
> So that night her parents leave and there she is. She turns on the radio and calls her dog into the living room to keep her company, and everything is fine. Then, just as her favorite song ends, a news bulletin comes on the radio. A killer has escaped from the insane asylum outside of town; he's at large, he's extremely dangerous, and nobody should go outside if they can at all help it lest he get them. The girl tries to tell herself that she has nothing to worry about

because her dog will protect her, but after that she's really creeped out and she decides to just go to bed.

Her dog always sleeps under her bed, and tonight is no exception. As she's drifting off to sleep, she sticks her hand under the bed and he licks it. So she feels a bit less scared.

A while later she wakes up to this weird dripping sound. She can't figure out what it is, and she's a bit more scared, but she sticks her hand under the bed again and the dog licks it again, so she goes back to sleep.

But later the noise wakes her up again: DRIP, DRIP, DRIP! Once more she sticks her hand under the bed, and her dog licks it, so she feels better and starts to go back to sleep. But the dripping noise is really bothering her, and she still can't fall asleep. She gets up and checks like every faucet in the house, but none of them are dripping. She does notice, however, that she can't hear it in the living room, so she decides to sleep on the couch.

She goes back to her room to get her pillow, and calls her dog to come out from under the bed, but he doesn't come. She bends down and looks under her bed, and she sees . . .

THE ESCAPED KILLER! He's holding her dying dog in his arms. He'd ripped its jaw off to keep it from barking, and its blood is going all over the floor. DRIP, DRIP, DRIP!

Sara's story has elements of several typical horror urban legends (I define the term "urban legend" more formally below). There's the radio's warning of an escaped maniac (as in "The Hook"), the home-alone theme, the violent crime, the ghoulish behavior, and especially the oral transmission of this "true" story down through the generations, complete with spooky sound effects. But something's missing from the usual versions of "The Licked Hand" (as folklorists call this legend). There should be a note written in blood that sums up the horror.

Here's one such version, as a Utah State University student told it to me during a folklore conference I attended there a few years ago. You must imagine a group of adolescent girls huddled together during a sleepover (or slumber party, if you prefer), scaring themselves by telling this little chiller:

> There was a blind woman who had a Seeing Eye dog, and her sighted roommate left her once for the night, reminding her to be careful because some convicts had escaped from a nearby prison. The blind woman went to sleep with her dog beside her bed, and during the night she thought she heard some noise.
>
> To comfort herself she put her hand down and felt a lick on her hand. In the morning her roommate returned and found the dog slashed to death, and the apartment had been robbed.
>
> Written in blood on the mirror were the words "HUMANS CAN LICK TOO."

You've probably figured out by now that stories like this can be told in endless variations. (The Seeing Eye dog is an unusual detail, probably inserted by the teller to justify having a dog in the room.) But that's not the end of the possible changes; here's another, rather mixed version of the story, coming also, as it happens, from Utah State University, and as reprinted in a folklore collection:

> A girl was babysitting the three children of her neighbors. Before the mom left, she told her to keep the

doors locked and the family dog close to her all the time they were gone. The dog would protect her and lick her hand from his regular spot behind the couch. The babysitter put the three little children to bed, went to the kitchen to get a snack, and returned to the living room to watch TV. She then noticed that the back door had been blown open which scared her because she thought the mom had locked her in. Nothing seemed out of the ordinary so she went back to wait for the kids' parents. Then the phone rang. A man on the other end said, "you had better go check the kids." She thought it was a prank call, but she checked to see if the guard dog was still with her to protect her. He was. The call came three more times, and finally, the girl decided to check the kids. When she reached the top of the stairs, there were the three children mutilated, the dog was butchered, and a bloody axe was there beside them. When she ran downstairs to call the police, "Humans can lick, too" was written in blood on the glass coffee table right in front of where she had been sitting. The murderer had been licking her hand ever since she had gone to the kitchen to get her snack. (Simon J. Bronner, *American Children's Folklore* [Little Rock, Ark.: August House, 1988], p. 151, quoted from a fourteen-year-old girl interviewed by a USU student for a folklore class in 1984)

If you recognize the opening of that version that's because it's from another scary UL, a favorite of the babysitting age-group, usually called "The Babysitter and the Man Upstairs," which often has the repeated line in a spooky voice, "Haaaaave yoooou checked the chillldren?" Such stories are constantly shifting and recombining, so "The Licked Hand," as we have seen, although often defined by the presence of the bloody note, doesn't necessarily need that detail. I've heard versions where the dog's slashed body, or sometimes just the dog's head, was found hanging in the bathroom going "DRIP, DRIP, DRIP," with or without a note written in blood on the shower door saying, "Humans [or "people"] can lick too," or "Not only dogs can lick," or some other similar line.

A common college dorm shocker is similar; it has the gore on the floor, a murdered girl, and a note, but no doggy. Here's one version of this "Roommate's Death" legend, told recently by an Eastern University student:

> About ten years ago on a college campus in Virginia a really freaky incident happened. Two roommates were out at a party and one decided to go home early because she was tired. She came home to find a stranger in her room with an axe in his hand. He killed her and laid her down in her bed. Well, the other roommate came home and decided not to turn the light on, so she wouldn't wake up her roommate. When she woke up the next morning she rolled over, only to see her dead roommate. As she was frantically running out of the room, she saw a message written on the mirror in blood: AREN'T YOU GLAD YOU DIDN'T TURN ON THE LIGHT!?

I've collected variations of that same basic story from all over the map, and it's usually localized. A student from Berea College, in Kentucky, told me the students there say it happened on their own campus, except for those who swear it happened at Eastern Kentucky University, in Richmond, or at the University of Kentucky, in Lexington. A student from Illinois State University, in Normal, wrote me that it had happened to a friend of a friend at Eastern Illinois University, in Charleston, while an Ohio State University student heard the same story, except that the roommate had been chopped up into teeny tiny pieces with an ax. (A dormitory R.A. [resident adviser] told freshmen that version to underscore the importance of locking their doors.) A young man in the college community of Spearfish, South Dakota, wrote me that when it is told there the events are supposed to have happened somewhere in North Dakota; but when he was attending South Dakota State University, at the other end of the state, the events were said to have happened in Minnesota or Kansas. Just as Daniel Defoe recognized centuries ago (see the first selection in the Chapter 1), such horror yarns may preserve the same basic plot elements, but when told they are most commonly attributed to somewhere other than the narrator's home turf.

I could go on just with variations of this gore-on-the-floor group of horror ULs, except that the more versions you hear or read, the less scary they may seem, and eventually you begin to anticipate the conclusions and the punch lines. On the other hand, more texts of these stories would allow us to wallow in some of the truly bizarre details that sometimes appear, like the versions in which the killer licks the victim's *feet*, or the ones in which the college roommate hears moaning and heavy breathing from the other side of the darkened room and pulls the pillow over her head, assuming that her roommate is entertaining a boyfriend that night. The climax—of the *story*, that is—may be something like, "There was her roommate, still in her bed, with seven knives sticking out of her chest and blood all over the sheets, and written on the mirror in blood was . . . " Well, you can finish that one yourself. (The discerning fan of ULs will notice that the motif of the handwriting on the wall [or door, or coffee table, or mirror, etc.] shows up again years later in the story of "AIDS Mary," a version of which is included in Chapter 8.)

The foregoing texts define "urban legend" by example,

and many more examples follow in this book. But first, for the promised formal definition, I quote here what I wrote in the introduction of a recent compilation:

> Urban legends (ULs) are true stories that are too good to be true. These popular fables describe presumably real (though odd) events that happened to a friend of a friend. And they are usually told by credible persons narrating them in a believable style because they *do* believe them. The settings and actions in ULs are realistic and familiar—homes, offices, hotels, shopping malls, freeways, etc.—and the human characters in urban legends are quite ordinary people. However, the bizarre, comic, or horrifying incidents that occur to these people go one step too far to be believable. (*Too Good to Be True: The Colossal Book of Urban Legends* [New York: W. W. Norton, 1999], p. 19)

Two more observations should be made about ULs, and specifically horror ones, before diving into more scary, creepy, shivery stories. First, although these legends belong to an old folkloric oral tradition, modern life and electronic communication are no barriers to their transmission. To the contrary, whatever decline there may have been in the oral telling and retelling of ULs has been more than replaced by their circulation on the great electronic grapevine of the Internet. And, somehow, they seem just as scary popping up on your computer screen as they do when told under dim lighting conditions at a sleepover, on a camping trip, at a dormitory bull session, or at a Halloween party.

The second point is that ULs do not have to be logical to be scary. Nobody ever questions such details as whether a human's lick could easily be mistaken for a dog's lick, whether ripping off a dog's jaw would silence the animal (or if, indeed, whether it would even be possible to do this without alerting the victims), whether prison or asylum escapees would head directly for a young female who is home alone, and especially whether essentially the same gory crimes could have occurred in so many different places without being reported by news media.

The purpose of this collection of horror ULs is not to raise such questions, nor to trace the horror plots through history and across geography (although that could be attempted), but rather simply to provide the enjoyment of a good scare while noting a few underlying lessons: Avoid being home alone! Remember to check the children! Double-check the doggy's lick! Turn on the light! And, above all, don't turn a deaf ear to warnings! That's really what urban legends are—warnings. And I warn you that some of them are pretty grotesque and terrifying. Although, by definition, these stories are not literally true, they do at least raise the possibility of something that might really have happened. But only to a FOAF, of course.

PRECURSORS

Before radio and television, long before the Internet and e-mail, and even before there were folklorists around to collect them, rumors and legends circulated in urban settings, and they were sometimes noted and documented by journalists and other writers. These precursors to modern urban legends—often horror stories—can sometimes even be traced back to ancient times, as were the accounts of supposed atrocities performed in the name of religion that folklorist Bill Ellis found to be "just as lively in the streets of pre-Christian Rome as they are in New York or Chicago today" (see Bill Ellis, "*De Legendis urbis*: Modern Legends in Ancient Rome," *Journal of American Folklore* 96 [1983]: pp. 200–208). The American author Nathaniel Hawthorne found an apt metaphor for such stories in his 1851 novel *The House of the Seven Gables* when in the opening chapter he described bloody rumors about a local murder as being typical of "stories . . . which are sure to spring up around such an event . . . and which, as in the present case, sometimes prolong themselves for ages afterwards, like the toadstools that indicate where the fallen and buried trunk of a tree has long since mouldered into the earth." We must also credit Hawthorne with recognizing the role of media in circulating rumors and legends, for he wrote in the same chapter about "Tradition—which sometimes brings down truth that history has let slip, but is oftener the wild babble of the time, such as was formerly spoken at the fireside, and now congeals in newspapers. . . . "

Those who recorded precursors to urban legends, whether they reported them simply as weird news or transmuted them into creative fiction, invariably rewrote the stories instead of publishing the basic oral versions as told on the streets. The early writers paraphrased, retold, and sometimes wildly elaborated on these stories, adding specific names for characters, background details, atmospheric touches, and even commentary. Yet some writers, as in the first three stories in this chapter, conveyed the horror of a situation without burying it in sentimentality or opinion. Among the elaborated stories in this chapter, Alexander Woollcott's "The Vanishing Lady" is especially flowery, and Bennett Cerf 's two New York City stories are not far behind. (I left out Carl Carmer's well-known literary treatment of "The Vanishing Hitchhiker" as being overly melodramatic for modern tastes and thus hardly scary at all.) The report of Dr. S. Weir Mitchell's first-person account of a ghost visitation and the claimed verbatim versions of the "Corpse in the Car" stories reported by Marie Bonaparte are much closer to the ideal of unvarnished texts now preferred by folklore scholars. At the end of the chapter I include examples of twentieth-century folkloristic and journalistic versions of "Embalmed Alive" and "The Vanishing Hitchhiker" as a transition to horror urban legends as they are usually told nowadays. I have also scattered a few more precursors among the modern legends in subsequent chapters.

The favorite scary urban legends of early writers tended to be supernatural (an uncommon trait in modern ULs), and the writers favored plots featuring corpses, cemeteries, damsels in distress, helpful strangers, devoted doctors and priests, gypsies, sudden deaths, insanity, nightmares, disease, and other such details. The settings tended to be lonely spots late at night, places with a dark and sometimes even romantic atmosphere and, if possible, with a hint of some terrible conspiracy. Yet, even in the earliest versions, there are previews of modern life in the mention of cars, hotels, elevators, the police, morticians, and the like. Some of the more traditional folkloristic details (or "motifs," as folklorists call them) were prophecies, the identification of a ghost in a portrait, mysterious sudden disappearances, and remarkable events occurring on the anniversary of a death.

As with all folk narratives circulating in oral tradition, there are some rather odd details to be found in these legends. Note, for example, the reference to a prophetic ritual in the 1941 version of "The Graveyard Wager," as well as those curious ten suitcases and ten coats left behind in the 1940 version of "The Vanishing Hitchhiker." Still, in their essentials, these precursors anticipate modern ULs: they are often attributed to FOAFs, exist in several versions, are unverified although told as true, and tend to be localized, even if the same story is known in many other places. Indeed, most of these precursor legends continue to be told today as modern ULs, updated for the present. Nowadays, however, the style of narration is more concise, less emotional, and includes stark and often rather abrupt endings. A major component of the horror of these ULs lies in the style of oral performance (or, in the Internet versions, verbal skill), a feature you will largely have to imagine while reading them. My recommendation is that you retell the legends in your own style after you have read them on the antiseptic printed page.

The legends in this chapter span three centuries, starting with Daniel Defoe's eighteenth-century journalistic treatment of plague stories and ending with twentieth-century versions of the classic ghost story "The Vanishing Hitchhiker." We realize in reading the first story that Defoe had it exactly right over three centuries ago when he pointed out that the events described are always supposed to have happened locally, although not exactly where the teller lives, that their essential details remain fixed wherever they are told, and that there are few if any reliable details mentioned in the stories. Furthermore, just as the Russian reporters learned in 1890 (see the third story), it is futile to attempt to track down an original source, much less the "truth" about a rumor or legend. As Defoe put it, "there was more of Tale than of Truth in those Things."

"Frightful Stories"

We had at this Time a great many frightful Stories told us of Nurses and Watchmen, who looked after the dying People, *that is to say*, hir'd Nurses, who attended infected People, using them barbarously, starving them smothering them, or by other wicked Means, hastening their End, *that is to say*, murthering of them: And Watchmen being set to guard Houses that were shut up, when there has been but one person left, and perhaps, that one lying sick, that they have broke in and murthered that Body, and immediately thrown them out into the Dead-Cart! And so they have gone scarce cold to the Grave.

I cannot say, but that some such Murthers were committed, and I think two were sent to Prison for it, but died before they could be try'd; and I have heard that three others, at several Times, were excused for Murthers of that kind; but I must say I believe nothing of its being so common a Crime, as some have since been pleas'd to say. . . .

. . . as for murthers, I do not find that there was ever any Proof of the Facts, in the manner, as it has been reported, *except as above.*

They did tell me indeed of a Nurse in one place, that laid a wet Cloth upon the Face of a dying Patient, who she tended, and so put an End to his Life, who was just expiring before: And another that smother'd a young Woman she was looking to, when she was in a fainting fit, and would have come to her self: Some that kill'd them by giving them one Thing, some another, and some starved them by giving them nothing at all: But these Stories had two Marks of Suspicion that always attended them, which caused me always to slight them, and to look on them as meer Stories, that People continually frighted one another with. (1.) That wherever it was that we heard it, they always placed the Scene at the farther End of the town, opposite, or most remote from where you were to hear it: If you heard it in *White-Chapel*, it had happened *at St. Giles's*, or at *Westminister*, or *Holborn*, or that End of the Town; if you heard of it at that End of the Town, then it was done in *White-Chapel*, or the *Minories*, or about *Cripplegate Parish*: If you heard of it in the City, why, then it had happened in *Southwark*; and if you heard of it in *Southwark*, then it was done in the City, and the like.

In the next Place, of what Part soever you heard the Story, the Particulars were always the same, especially that of laying a wet double Clout on a dying Man's Face, and that of smothering a young Gentlewoman; so that it was apparent, at least to my Judgment, that there was more of Tale than of Truth in those Things.

From Daniel Defoe, A Journal of the Plague Year, *Norton Critical Edition, ed. by Paula R. Backscheider (New York: W. W. Norton, 1992), pp. 70–72.*

"The Rat-Dog"

Two ladies, friends of a near relative of my own, from whom I received an account of the circumstance, were walking in Regent Street, and were accosted by a man who requested them to buy a beautiful little dog, covered with long, white hair, which he carried in his arms. Such things are not uncommon in that part of London, and the ladies passed on without heeding him. He followed, and repeated his entreaties, stating that as it was the last he had to sell, they should have it at a reasonable price. They looked at the animal; it was really an exquisite little creature, and they were at last persuaded. The man took it home for them, received his money, and left the dog in the arms of one of the ladies. A short time elapsed, and the dog, which had been very quiet in spite of a restless, bright eye, began to show symptoms of uneasiness, and as he ran about the room, exhibited some unusual movements, which rather alarmed the fair purchasers. At last, to their great dismay, the new dog ran squeaking up one of the window curtains; so that when the gentleman of the house returned home a few minutes after, he found the ladies in consternation, and right glad to have his assistance. He vigorously seized the animal, took out his penknife, cut off its covering, and displayed a large rat to their astonished eyes, and of course to its own destruction.

From Sarah Bowditch, Anecdotes of the Habits and Instincts of Animals, *5th ed. (London: Grant and Griffith, 1891), pp. 216–17; first published 1852. More than a century later friends of friends were still telling versions of this story as "The Mexican Pet"; see Chapter 4 for another version.*

"The Ghost in Search of (Spiritual) Help"

There is a story going about town [St. Petersburg, Russia] that is worthy of attention. The only question is whether it is true, and to what extent. The other day, somewhere on Sergievskaya Street, or near it, a priest carrying the holy sacraments came to a certain apartment after mass. A young man answered the door.

"I was asked to come here and give the sacraments to a sick man," said the priest.

"You must have made a mistake. Nobody lives here except me."

"No, a lady came up to me today and gave me this very address and asked me to give the sacraments to the man who lives here."

The young apartment dweller was perplexed.

"Why, look, that is the very woman who asked me to come," said the priest, pointing to a woman's portrait hanging on the wall.

"That is the portrait of my dead mother."

Awe, fear, terror seized hold of the young man. Under the impression of all this he took communion.

That evening he lay dead.

Such is the story.

• • •

When the story reached me about the unusual event that had happened to one of the Petersburg priests, my interest was aroused not so much by the question of its probability as by the question [of] just where the rumor got started, how it spread, and finally how it became common property and even turned up in the columns of minor newspapers. . . .

The story about the miracle became more and more persistent and appeared in a thousand versions. Surely, I thought, those with whom it originated and whom it concerns above all will come forth with frank and exact explanations, so as to remove temptation from those who love to lie, and put an end to the gossip, which is becoming more and more absurd. . . .

I resolved to make an effort to find the evidence in this chaos of rumor, to track down the starting point of the tales, their primary source, and in this way to get an explanation. . . .

[The story is retold, with accounts of the many variations.]

That is what they are telling.

If the tale named names, the whole matter would be quite different. Everybody would naturally believe the word of the priest who played one of the active roles in this unfathomable story.

But up to the present time not a single priest has made any statement in print about this interesting occurrence. It is said that the priest himself told a certain lady, she told three of her acquaintances, and so on. . . .

I made the rounds of dozens of houses, talked with pious, mystery-bearing old women, with mysterious tight-lipped old men, with doorkeepers and janitors—in a word, with everybody who in one way or another "knew something."

. . . despite my sincerest desire and all possible efforts, I have found no evidence for this story.

It is true that at one time it looked as if I might have in my hands that enigmatic "final link"; at least the tale led me to a certain priest. But since he informed me bluntly that he didn't know anything about anything, there is no point in calling attention to him.

Still the rumor keeps growing. Talk about the miracle is going on in almost every house. Just what does this mean?

Two suppositions inevitably arise: either there are people

who know the truth, have the facts in their hands, and are keeping silent—or else the tale about the miracle is one of those stupid rumors that spring up nobody knows where and find a wide audience only in the kind of society that wanders in darkness, and in which there thrives a tendency toward superstition, if not outright witchcraft, instead of healthy, sober thinking.

From two St. Petersburg newspapers published in December 1890, as translated by William B. Edgerton in "The Ghost in Search of Help for a Dying Man," Journal of the Folklore Institute *5 (1968): pp. 32–36.*

"The Ghost in Search of (Medical) Help"

One day in February, 1949, Dr. Philip Cook of Worcester, Mass., while on a visit to New York City, told me this story which he had heard the famous [Philadelphia] doctor and writer S. Weir Mitchell tell at a medical meeting years ago. (Dr. Mitchell [born 1829] died in 1914.)

"I was sitting in my office late one night when I heard a knock and, going to the door, found a little girl crying, who asked me to go at once to her home to visit a very sick patient. I told her that I was practically retired and never made evening calls, but she seemed to be in such great distress that I agreed to make the call and so wrote down the name and address she gave me. So I got my bag, hat, and coat, and returned to the door, but the little girl was gone. However, I had the address and so went on and made the call. When I got there, a woman came to the door in tears. I asked if there was a patient needing attention. She said that there had been—her little daughter—but that she had just died.

She then invited me in. I saw the patient lying dead in her bed, and it was the little girl who had called at my office."

From R. W. G. Vail, "A Philadelphia Variant of the Hitchhiking Ghost," New York Folklore Quarterly *6 (1950): p. 254; also quoted in my study of numerous versions of this classic ghost story in* The Truth Never Stands in the Way of a Good Story.

"The Vanishing Lady"

As I first heard the story, it began with the arrival from Marseilles of an Englishwoman and her young, inexperienced daughter, a girl of seventeen or thereabouts. The mother was the frail, pretty widow of an English officer who had been stationed in India, and the two had just come from Bombay, bound for home. In the knowledge that, after reaching there, she would soon have to cross to Paris to sign some papers affecting her husband's estate, she decided at the last minute to shift her passage to a Marseilles steamer, and, by going direct to Paris, look up the lawyers there and finish her business before crossing the Channel to settle forever and a day in the Warwickshire village where she was born.

Paris was so tumultuously crowded for the Exposition that they counted themselves fortunate when the *cocher* desposited them at the Crillon, and they learned that their precautionary telegram from Marseilles had miraculously caught a room on the wing—a double room with a fine, spacious sitting-room looking out on the Place de la Concorde. I could wish that they had wired one of those less magnificent caravansaries, if only that I might revel again in such a name as the Hotel of Jacob and of England, or, better still, the Hotel of the Universe and of

Portugal. But, as the story reached me, it was to the Crillon that they went.

The long windows of their sitting-room gave on a narrow, stone-railed balcony and were half-shrouded in heavy curtains of plum-colored velvet. As again and again the girl later on had occasion to describe the look of that room when first she saw it, the walls were papered in old rose. A high-backed sofa, an oval satinwood table, a mantel with an ormolu clock that had run down—these also she recalled.

The girl was the more relieved that there would be no need of a house-to-house search for rooms, for the mother had seemed unendurably exhausted from the long train ride, and was now of such a color that the girl's first idea was to call the house physician, hoping fervently that he spoke English, for neither she nor her mother spoke any French at all.

The doctor, when he came—a dusty, smelly little man with a wrinkled face lost in a thicket of whiskers, and a reassuring Legion of Honor ribbon in the buttonhole of his lapel—did speak a little English. After a long, grave look and a few questions put to the tired woman on the bed in the shaded room, he called the girl into the sitting-room and told her frankly that her mother's condition was serious; that it was out of the question for them to think of going on to England next day; that on the morrow she might better be moved to a hospital, etc., etc.

All these things he would attend to. In the meantime he wanted the girl to go at once to his home and fetch him a medicine that his wife would give her. It could not be as quickly prepared in any chemist's. Unfortunately, he lived on the other side of Paris and had no telephone, and with all Paris *en fête* it would be perilous to rely on any messenger. Indeed, it would be a saving of time and worry if she could go, armed with a note to his wife he was even then scribbling in French at a desk in the sitting-room. In the lobby below, the manager of the hotel, after an excited colloquy with the doctor, took charge of her most sympathetically, himself putting her into a *sapin* and, as far as she could judge, volubly directing the driver how to reach a certain house in the Rue Val du Grâce, near the Observatoire.

It was then that the girl's agony began, for the ramshackle victoria crawled through the festive streets and, as she afterwards realized, more often than not crawled in the wrong direction. The house in the Rue Val du Grâce seemed to stand at the other end of the world, when the carriage came at last to a halt in front of it. The girl grew old in the time which passed before any answer came to her ring at the bell. The doctor's wife, when finally she appeared, read his note again and again, then with much muttering and rattling of keys stationed the girl in an airless waiting room and left her there so long that she was weeping for very desperation, before the medicine was found, wrapped, and turned over to her.

A hundred times during that wait she rose and started for the door, determined to stay no longer but to run back empty-handed through the streets to her mother's bedside. A thousand times in the wretched weeks that followed she loathed herself for not having obeyed that impulse, but always there was the feeling that having come so far and having waited so long, she must not leave without the medicine just for lack of the strength of will to stick it out a little longer—perhaps only a few minutes longer.

Then the snail's pace trip back to the Right Bank was another nightmare, and it ended only when, at the *cocher's* mulish determination to deliver her to some hotel in the Place Vendôme, she leaped to the street and in sheer terror appealed for help to a passing young man whose alien tweeds and boots told her he was a compatriot of hers.

He was still standing guard beside her five minutes later when, at long last, she arrived at the desk of the Crillon and called for her key, only to have the very clerk who had handed her a pen to register with that morning look at her without recognition and blandly ask, "Whom does Mademoiselle wish to see?" At that a cold fear clutched her heart, a sudden surrender to a panic that she had fought back as preposterous when first it visited her as she sat and twisted her handkerchief in the waiting room of the doctor's office on the Left Bank; a panic born when, after the doctor had casually told her he had no telephone, she heard the fretful ringing of its bell on the other side of his walnut door.

This then was the predicament of the young English girl as she stood there at the desk of the hotel in Paris—a stranger in the city and a stranger to its bewildering tongue. She had arrived that morning from India and had left her ailing mother in charge of the house physician while she went out in quest of medicine for her—a quest in which, through a malignant conspiracy between perverse circumstances and apparently motiveless passers-by, she had lost four hours.

But now with the bottle of medicine clutched in her hand, she reached the hotel at last, only to be stared down by the clerk at the desk, only to have the very man who had shown them their rooms with such a flourish that morning now gaze at her opaquely as though she were some slightly demented creature demanding admission to someone else's apartment.

But, no, Mam'zelle must be mistaken. Was it not at some other hotel she was descended? Two more clerks came fluttering into the conference. They all eyed her without a flicker of recognition. Did Mam'zelle say her room was No. 342? Ah, but 342 was occupied by M. Quelquechose. Yes, a French client of long standing. He had been occupying it these past two weeks and more. Ah, no, it would be impossible to disturb him. All this while the lobby, full of hurrying, polyglot strangers, reeled around her.

She demanded the registration slips only to find in that

day's docket no sign of the one she herself had filled out that morning on their arrival, the while her tired mother leaned against the desk and told her how. And even as the clerk now shuffled the papers before her eyes, the stupefying bloodstone which she had noticed on his ring-finger when he handed her the pen five hours before, winked at her in confirmation.

From then on she came only upon closed doors. The same house physician who had hustled her off on her tragic wild-goose chase across Paris protested now with all the shrugs and gestures of his people that he had dispatched her on no such errand, that he had never been summoned to attend her mother, that he had never seen her before in all his life. The same hotel manager who had so sympathetically helped her into the carriage when she set forth on her fruitless mission, denied her now as flatly and somehow managed to do it with the same sympathetic solicitude, suggesting that Mam'zelle must be tired, that she should let them provide another chamber where she might repose herself until such time as she could recollect at what hotel she really belonged or until some inquiries should bring in news of where her mother and her luggage were, if—

For always there was in his ever polite voice the unspoken reservation that the whole mystery might be a thing of her own disordered invention. Then, and in the destroying days that followed, she was only too keenly aware that these evasive people—the personnel of the hotel, the attachés of the embassy, the reporters of the *Paris Herald*, the officials at the Sûreté—were each and every one behaving as if she had lost her wits. Indeed there were times when she felt that all Paris was rolling its eyes behind her back and significantly tapping its forehead.

Her only aid and comfort was the aforesaid Englishman who, because a lovely lady in distress had come up to him in the street and implored his help, elected thereafter to believe her against all the evidence which so impressed the rest of Paris. He proved a pillar of stubborn strength because he was some sort of well-born junior secretary at the British Embassy with influence enough to keep her agony from gathering dust in the official pigeon-holes.

His faith in her needed to be unreasoning because there slowly formed in his mind a suspicion that for some unimaginable reason all these people—the hotel attendants and even the police—were part of a plot to conceal the means whereby the missing woman's disappearance had been effected. This suspicion deepened when, after a day's delay, he succeeded in forcing an inspection of Room 342 and found that there was no detail of its furnishing which had not been altered from the one etched into the girl's memory.

It remained to him to prove the mechanism of that plot and to guess at its invisible motive—a motive strong enough to enlist all Paris in the silent obliteration of a woman of no importance, moreover a woman who, as far as her daughter knew, had not an enemy in the world. It was the purchased confession of one of the paper-hangers, who had worked all night in the hurried transformation of Room 342, that started the unraveling of the mystery.

By the time the story reached me, it had lost all its content of grief and become as unemotional as an anagram. Indeed, a few years ago it was a kind of circulating parlor game and one was challenged to guess what had happened to the vanished lady. Perhaps you yourself have already surmised that the doctor had recognized the woman's ailment as a case of the black plague smuggled in from India; that his first instinctive step, designed only to give time for spiriting her out of the threatened hotel, had, when she died that afternoon, widened into a conspiracy on the part of the police to suppress, at all costs to this one girl, an obituary notice which, had it ever leaked out, would have emptied

Paris overnight and spread ruin across a city that had gambled heavily on the great Exposition for which its gates were even then thrown wide.

From Alexander Woollcott, While Rome Burns *(New York: Viking Press, 1934), pp. 87–93. Woollcott, whose book was a best-seller, called this legend "a fair specimen of folklore in the making" and traced variants back to 1889 before reaching a dead end. "Quelquechose," the supposed name of the guest in Room 342, means merely "something" in French. Woollcott's long-winded and melodramatic retelling contrasts with the following brief "folk" version from England.*

"The Foreign Hotel"

A lady and her daughter were traveling abroad, and arrived late at night, very tired after an exhausting journey, at the hotel where they had booked their rooms. The mother was particularly worn out. They were put into adjoining rooms, and the daughter tumbled into bed and fell asleep at once. She slept long and heavily, and it was well on in the next day before she got up. She opened the door into her mother's room, and found it empty. And it was not the room into which they had gone the night before. The wallpaper was different, the furniture was different, the bed was made up. She rang, and got no answer to her bell; she dressed and went downstairs.

"Can you tell me where my mother is?" she said to the woman at the reception desk.

"Your mother, mademoiselle?"

"Yes, the lady who arrived with me last night."

"But, mademoiselle, you came alone."

"We booked in; the night porter will remember; we wrote for two rooms!"

"Mademoiselle indeed wrote for two rooms, but she arrived alone."

And wherever she asked among the servants she got the same answer, until she began to think that she must be mad.

At last she went back to England and told her friends what had happened and one of them went to investigate. He went to the consul and the police and at last he found out the truth. The mother had been more than tired when she arrived that night, she had been in the invasion stages of cholera. No sooner had she gone to bed than she was taken violently ill; the doctor was sent for, she died, and the hotel owners were filled with panic and decided to conceal all that had happened. The body was carried away, the furniture was taken out to be burnt, the wall was re-papered, and all the staff were told to allow nothing to be guessed of what had happened. They knew that not a guest would be left to them if it was known that cholera had been in the house.

From Katharine M. Briggs and Ruth L. Tongue, Folktales of England *(Chicago: University of Chicago Press, 1965), pp. 98–99. Collected by Briggs from a woman in Yorkshire in 1915.*

"The Corpse in the Car"

Soon after the Munich agreement had averted immediate war, a friend and fellow psycho-analyst, Dr. R. Loewenstein, told me the following story in the Autumn of 1938, a story he vouched for as true. I give it verbatim:

1. In September 1938, a young man who was expecting his call-up was driving his fiancée to Laval intending to leave her with relatives. Outside Paris he stops for petrol. A middle-aged couple ask where he is going and then beg a lift for the

lady who is going in that direction whereas the man is returning to Paris to join up the following day. As they drive, the fiancée begins to cry and talk about their imminent separation. The stranger, however, assures them all will be well and tells the girl to stop crying. "You'll never be called up," she says to the man, "because there won't be a war. Anyway Hitler will be dead in six months." This she repeats several times. At Laval, before taking leave of the young man she asks whether he intends to return to Paris, and when. He replies that he is returning immediately.

The lady then advises him not to drive back that night because, if he does, he will find a corpse in his car. The young people however think her dotty and drive off without asking either her name or address. Later, before he leaves Laval, the young man's relatives ask him to give a lift to a lad they know who is also expecting an immediate call-up. He agrees. En route, the passenger says he feels drowsy, stretches out on the back seat and falls asleep. Back in Paris, the car stops at the passenger's address, the young man opens the door to wake him and finds the lad dead. . . .

A year later, in Autumn 1939, when Hitler, contrary to the latter prediction, had lived long enough to plunge Europe into war, another story came my way, this time told by a masseur at the Turkish Baths in Paris to my husband, with similar assurances of authenticity. According to him, the incident had happened to the brother-in-law of another regular patron, whose name he gave. Here again is the text of the story as given me by the same masseur by telephone:

2. A man is called up. With his wife and daughter he drives to Versailles. It is late and he says to his wife: "I shan't have petrol enough to get up the hill." Two or three hundred metres from the top of the rise to St. Cloud, his tank runs dry. He gets out, looks right and left, but to no effect. Then, however, under the trees he sees some gypsies whom he calls to

help push the car uphill. One of these gypsies then says: "You won't get back to-night without a stiff in your car." He fills up with petrol and is returning to Paris when he is stopped by a policeman who asks him to take an injured man to hospital. Before they could reach the hospital, however, the injured man was dead in the car. But before this, the driver had said to the gypsy: "Since you're such a good prophet, can't you say when the war will end?" "In the Autumn," the latter had answered, "after tremendous events."

From Marie Bonaparte, Myths of War *(London: Imago Publishing, 1947), pp. 13–14. These are the first two of twenty-nine versions of the story from all across Europe and one from Boston that she studied. An American version of the story was reported in a letter to* Time, *published November 20, 1939, pp. 6–7.*

"The Graveyard Wager"

My grandfather and grandmother told me this, said Mr. Gregory, and they said it was a true story. They said there was a girl, and she wanted a sweetheart, and she wanted to know who she was going to marry. And the people told her, if you will go to the graveyard some night by yourself, and not tell nobody where you are going, and take a table fork with you and stick it down in a grave, you will see the man who you will marry. And in olden times the women wore long dresses, you know. So, she was afraid to go, but she kept thinking about it. So after a while she decided to go. So she went, and as she stooped down to stick the fork in the grave she stuck it through her dress. And she thought it was something pulling her down, and it scared her to death, and she died right there.

• • •

I grew up hearing this story in a small town in central Kentucky.

Several teenage girls were sleeping over at one girl's house while the girl's parents were away.

After the lights were out, they started talking about the recent burial of an old man in a nearby cemetery. A rumor was going around that the man had been buried alive, and had been heard trying to claw his way out.

One girl laughed at the idea. So the others dared her to get up and visit the grave. As proof that she had gone, she was to drive a wooden stake into the earth above the grave.

They sent their friend off and shut off the lights again, expecting her to return right away.

But an hour passed, and then another, without any sign of the girl. The others lay awake, gradually growing terrified. Morning came, and she still hadn't returned.

Later that day, the girl's parents arrived home, and parents and friends went together to the cemetery.

They found the girl lying on the grave—dead. When she squatted down to push the wooden stake into the ground, she drove it through the hem of her skirt. When she tried to stand up and couldn't, she thought the dead man had grabbed hold of her—and she died instantly of fright.

The first version was collected in 1941 by a worker for the Virginia Writer's Project of the WPA (Work Projects Administration) and published in Thomas E. Barden's Virginia Folk Legends *(Charlottesville and London: University Press of Virginia, 1991), p. 307. The second version was sent to me in 1987 by a woman in Bloomington, Indiana.*

"Room for One More"

An intelligent, comely New York girl of twenty-odd summers was invited for the first time to the Carolina estate of some distant relatives. She looked forward to the visit, and bought quite an extensive wardrobe with which to impress her Southern cousins.

The plantation fulfilled her fondest expectations. The grounds, the manor house, the relatives themselves were perfect. She was assigned to a room in the western wing, and prepared to retire for the night in a glow of satisfaction. Her room was drenched with the light of a full moon. Outside was a gravel roadway which curved up to the main entrance of the building.

Just as she was climbing into her bed, she was startled by the sound of horses' hooves on the gravel roadway. She walked to the window, and saw, to her astonishment, a magnificent old coach, drawn by four coal-black horses, pull up sharply directly in front of her window. The coachman jumped from his perch, looked up, and pointed a long, bony finger at her. He was hideous. His face was chalk white. A deep scar ran the length of his left cheek. His nose was beaked. As he pointed at her, he droned in sepulchral tones: "There is room for one more!" Then, as she recoiled in terror, the coach, the horses and the ominous coachman disappeared completely. The roadway stretched empty before her in the moonlight.

The girl slept little that night, but in the reassuring sunlight of the following morning, she was able to convince herself that the sight she had seen had been nothing more than a nightmare, or an obsession caused by a disordered stomach. She said nothing about it to her hosts.

The next night, however, provided an exact repetition of the first night's procedure. The same coach drove up the roadway.

ess. It was one of those anecdotes that everybody swore had actually happened to his first cousin or next-door neighbor, and several narrators got very testy when they were informed that several other people's cousins had evidently undergone the same experience a few weeks before.

At any rate, the legend maintained that a very lovely but poverty-stricken damsel was invited to a formal dance. It was her chance to enter a brand-new world. Who knew but what some rich young man would fall in love with her and lift her out of her life in a box factory? The catch in the matter was that she had no suitable dress to wear for such a great occasion.

"Why don't you rent a costume for the evening?" suggested a friend. She did. She went to a pawnshop near her little flat and for a surprisingly reasonable sum rented a beautiful white satin evening gown with all the accessories to match. Miraculously, it fit her like a glove, and she looked so radiant when she arrived at the party that she created a minor sensation. She was cut in on again and again, and as she whirled happily around the floor she felt that her luck indeed had changed for good.

Then she began to feel faint and nauseated. She fought against a growing discomfort as long as she could, but finally she stole out of the house and had just sufficient strength to stagger into a cab and creep up the stairs to her room. She threw herself onto her bed, broken-hearted, and it was then, possibly in her delirium, that she heard a woman's voice whispering into her ear. It was harsh and bitter. "Give me back my dress," it said. "Give me back my dress! It belongs to the dead. . . . "

The next morning the lifeless body of the young girl was found stretched out on her bed. The unusual circumstances led the coroner to order an autopsy. The girl had been poisoned by embalming fluid, which had entered her pores when she grew overheated from dancing. The pawnbroker was reluctant to

The same coachman pointed to her and croaked

for one more!" Then the entire equipage disapp

The girl, in complete panic, could scarcely

ing. She trumped up some excuse to her hos

back to New York. Her doctor had an office on

floor of a modern medical center. She taxied t

station, and told him her story in tremulous tor

The doctor's matter-of-fact acceptance of

much to quiet her nerves. He persuaded her

been the victim of a peculiar hallucination, la

terror, kissed her paternally on the brow, and dis

a state of infinite relief. She rang the bell for the

a door swung open before her.

The elevator was very crowded. She was abou

her way inside when a familiar voice rang in her

room for one more!" it said. The operator was th

who had pointed at her! She saw his chalk-wh

livid scar, the beaked nose! She drew back and sci

the elevator door banged shut in her face.

A moment later the building shook with a te

The elevator that had gone on without her broke

its cables and plunged eighteen stories to th

Everybody in it, of course, was crushed to a pulp.

From "The Current Crop of Ghost Stories," in Bennett Ce
Ghost Stories *(New York: Random House, Modern Librar*
351–53.

"The Poisoned Dress"

A favorite story of New York literary circles a few
concerned the beautiful young girl in the wh

admit that he knew where the dress came from, but spoke out when he heard that the District Attorney's office was involved. It had been sold him by an undertaker's assistant, who had taken it from the body of a dead girl just before the casket was nailed down for the last time.

Also from "The Current Crop of Ghost Stories," in Bennett Cerf's Famous Ghost Stories *(New York: Random House, Modern Library, 1944), pp. 359–60. Cerf wrote, "Several of them I heard more than once. The minor details varied, but the essentials were always the same. I have tried to keep the stories brief. It seems to me that they are more effective that way." His attempts to keep his tellings short and to the point are a far cry from the much more concise oral texts collected by folklorists.*

"Embalmed Alive"

My cousin's cousin, who works in Fine Women's Wear at Neiman Marcus in Beverly Hills, told me this "true" story last Thanksgiving.

He told me that since Neiman's has a very lenient return policy, many wealthy women put $10,000 dresses on their charge accounts, wear them once, have them dry-cleaned, and then return them to the store.

Someone at the store told him what happened because of this practice one time before he worked there. After a woman returned a very expensive designer dress, another woman bought the same dress and later broke out in a horrible rash while wearing it.

She went to a dermatologist, who said he had to treat her skin for exposure to formaldehyde, and so she sued Neiman's for the doctor's charge.

The store traced the dress to the first woman, who admitted that her mother had wanted to be buried in that dress. But the daughter didn't want to bury such an expensive dress, so she got it back from the mortician after the funeral service and returned it to the store.

The second woman had been exposed to formaldehyde that soaked into the fabric from the corpse.

I thought this was true until my girlfriend told me just the other day that her grandmother wouldn't let her buy dresses from thrift shops because of a woman who had died from formaldehyde in a second-hand dress.

So this hot new story turned out to be at least sixty years old!

From a letter sent to me by a reader in Los Angeles, California, in January 1992.

"A Pretty Girl in the Road"

One time there was a fellow a-riding along, and it was getting dark and looked like rain besides. He seen a girl a-standing beside the road, where an old house had burnt down but the chimney was still there. She was a tall slim girl with a poke bonnet on, but he seen her face plain. He stopped and says, "If you're going somewheres I will give you a ride, because my horse carries double." She says her name is Stapleton, and her folks live down the road a piece. So then she jumped up behind him light as a feather. Pretty soon he spurred the horse a little, so she had to put her arms round his waist.

They rode on about a mile and he found out her first name was Lucy, and she ain't married neither. He could feel her breath on his neck while they was a-talking, and he liked it fine. He got to thinking this was the kind of a girl he wanted to marry up with, and he liked her better than any girl he ever seen before.

So they rode another mile, and it was pretty dark by this time, and they come to a graveyard. And there was a big house with lights in the windows just a little way off. She says, "That's where my folks live, but I'd better get down here." He figured she was going to take a short cut home, so her paw wouldn't know she had been riding with a stranger. Folks was awful particular about what their daughters done in them days. The girl jumped off and walked over to the gate. He says, "I'll be seeing you pretty soon," but Lucy just waved him goodbye and went into the graveyard.

The fellow waited a while so she would have time to get home, and then he rode up in front of the big house. Soon as the dogs begun to bark an old man come out, and he says: "My name is Stapleton." He says the fellow is welcome to have supper with them and stay all night, as they have got plenty of room. And then he hollered a boy out of the barn to take care of the traveler's horse.

They had a good supper, but there wasn't nobody at the table only Judge Stapleton and his wife. The fellow kept look- ing for Lucy to show up any minute, but she never come. So after while he went to bed in the spare room, and it was a fine shuck mattress, but he didn't sleep very good.

Next morning after breakfast they got to talking, and the Judge says him and his wife just moved here a year ago. "We used to live two miles down the road," he says, "but our house was lightnin'-struck and burnt plumb down. There ain't noth- ing left now but the old chimney." The traveler says yes, he seen that chimney when he rode by there last night. "I didn't mind losing the house," says the Judge, "only our daughter was sick in bed. We carried her out to the gate, but the shock was too much for her, and she died that same night."

The fellow just set there, and the Judge went on a-talking about what a fine girl his daughter was, and how him and the old woman was pretty lonesome nowadays. "We buried her in that little graveyard," says the Judge. "You can see her stone from the front gallery. There ain't a day goes by, rain or shine, that my wife don't walk over there and set by the grave a while."

Everything was mighty still for a minute, and then the traveler says: "What was your daughter's name?" It sounded kind of funny the way he said it, but he was obliged to know.

"Her name was Lucy," says the Judge.

From Vance Randolph, "Folktales from Arkansas," Journal of American Folklore 65 (1952): pp. 163–64. This is, of course, the "Vanishing Hitchhiker" legend in an early rural version. Randolph's note to the story reads, "Told by Mr. Tom Shiras, Mountain Home, Ark., September, 1941. He said it was a 'foolish ghost story' popular at Mountain Home about 1930."

"The Vanishing Hitchhiker"

(This story was told to the narrator by a man who said he knew the boys concerned very well.) These boys went to a public dance. It was in a small town and they knew most of the people there. They saw a very attractive girl in a white dress, and one of the boys asked her to dance with him. Her hands were so cold that he thought she was ill. However, after the dance was over they offered to take the girl home and she consented. They got into the car and she gave them her address. But when they got to the Oak Ridge Cemetery the girl said, "I forgot. I promised I'd get out here."

The boys saw her go through a hedge. They waited, but

she didn't come back. They went into the cemetery and looked around but found nothing. They saw a man and a woman leaving, but couldn't find the girl. Worried, they went to the address she had given them. The people there said, "Are you sure she gave you this address?" They showed the boys some pictures and the boys recognized the girl at the dance. "That's even the dress she was wearing," they said. Then the people told them that the girl was their daughter and that she had died two years ago. This happening preyed so on one of the boy's minds that he went to the Elgin hospital for the insane and died about six months later.

• • •

A man and his wife were driving home from a party late in the evening. The road was dark and deserted. Suddenly in the beam of the headlights they saw a girl standing at the side of the road—a suitcase in one hand and her coat in the other. Being fearful for the girl's safety on that dark, deserted road, they stopped the car and insisted that she ride with them. Without a word she got into the car and they rode on. Very few words were spoken. They rode in silence for about half an hour. The man, to break the silence, turned and asked where she lived so he could take her home. But she had disappeared, leaving suitcase and coat. The man swears he was doing from thirty-five to forty miles an hour: so she couldn't have jumped out.

On the suitcase was an address. They went to this address and met an elderly woman of, say, sixty years of age. They explained what had happened; she told them that they were the tenth persons who had brought her a suitcase and a coat and showed them nine other suitcases and coats of the same design in a closet. She told them the girl was her daughter who had died a long time ago at the age of sixteen.

The man's wife, being a nervous type of person, took sick

immediately afterward and was committed to an insane asylum. He nearly went wacky himself. I heard this story about two years ago and it's still going around. I asked my friend if he had heard it and he said he'd heard it in Pennsylvania, but differently worded.

The first version is text No. 15 from Richard K. Beardsley and Rosalie Hankey, "The Vanishing Hitchhiker," California Folklore Quarterly *1 (1942): p. 325, collected from North Riverside, Illinois, in 1939. The second version is text No. 5 from the same source, this one collected from Ossining, New York, in 1940.*

"Girl at the Underpass"

Not long ago, but before interstate highways ran around towns and cities, a young man left Greensboro late one night to drive to his home in Lexington. At that time, just east of Jamestown, the old road dipped through a tunnel under the train tracks. The young man knew the road well, but it was a thick foggy night in early summer and he drove cautiously, especially when he neared the Jamestown underpass. Many wrecks had taken place at that spot. He slowed down on the curve leading to the tunnel and was halfway through it when his eyes almost popped out of his head. Standing on the roadside just beyond the underpass was an indistinct white figure with arm raised in a gesture of distress. The young man quickly slammed on his brakes and came to a stop beside the figure.

It was a girl, young, beautiful, resplendent in a long white evening dress. Her troubled eyes were glaring straight toward him. Obviously she was in need. He jumped from the car and ran around to where she stood motionless. "Can I help you?"

"Yes." Her voice was low, strange. "I want to go home. I live in High Point."

He opened the door, and she got in. As they drove off, he said, "I'm glad I came by. I didn't expect to find anyone like you on the road so late at night."

"I was at a dance." She spoke in a monotone. "My date and I had a quarrel. It was very bad. I made him drop me back there."

He tried to continue the conversation, but she would say nothing more until they were into High Point. "Turn at the next left," she said. "I live three doors on the right." He parked before a darkened house, got out of the car and went around to open the door for her. There was no one there! He looked into the back seat. No one! He thought she might have rushed up the sidewalk and out of sight.

Confused and undecided what to do next, he thought it only reasonable to find out if she had entered the house. He went up the steps and knocked on the door. No one came. He knocked again. There was no sound anywhere. After a third knock, through the side panes a dim light appeared from the pitch-black hallway. Finally the door was opened by a white-haired woman in a night robe.

"I brought a girl to this house," he explained, "but now I can't find her. Have you seen her? I picked her up out on the highway."

"Where?"

"At the Jamestown underpass. She told me she had been to a dance and was on her way home."

"Yes, I know," said the woman wearily. "That was my daughter. She was killed in a wreck at that tunnel five years ago tonight. And every year since, on this very night, she signals a young man like you to pick her up. She is still trying to get home."

The young man turned from the doorway, speechless. The

dim light in the house went out. He drove on to Lexington, but never has he forgotten, nor will he ever forget, the beautiful hitchhiker and how she vanished into the night.

From Richard Walser, North Carolina Legends *(Raleigh: North Carolina Department of Cultural Resources, Division of Archives and History, 1980), pp. 60–61.*

CHILLS UP YOUR SPINE

The precursors in Chapter 1 prove that scary urban legends have been told for ages. It took a long while, however, for modern folklorists to recognize this rich vein of contemporary tradition. Oblivious of the scholars' work, twentieth-century folk simply continued to scare themselves silly by telling these "true" stories that sent chills up their spines. And the tradition continues, despite decades of debunkings: while some past urban legends have been reduced to joke status or survive only as memories of naive adolescent belief, other scary legends thrive, even in the age of the Internet.

Folklorists of the 1940s and 1950s began to collect "urban belief tales," first from their students at colleges and universities; they unearthed a hugely popular repertoire of shockers about marauding hook men, campus killers, terrified babysitters, women attacked driving alone at night, poisoned dresses, fraternity hazing pranks gone awry, and other such gruesome themes. Texts of these stories, eventually dubbed "urban legends," first appeared in the regional folklore journals of the time, then eventually in the standard indexes of folk-narrative plots and motifs. A typical entry in Indiana University professor Ernest Baughman's *Type and Motif Index of the Folktales of*

England and North America (1966) reduces an early horror UL to motif number N384.0.1.1, summarizing it like this:

> *The cadaver arm.* Medical students (or student nurses or hospital employees) play a trick on one of their number by suspending a cadaver arm or leg from the light cord in the person's room (sometimes the object is placed in the person's bed). Some circumstance keeps them from being on hand to observe the person's reaction; the next day they remember the joke and go to the victim's room to investigate. They have to break down the door. They find the victim sitting on the bed—her hair is snow white—and she is gnawing on the cadaver arm.

This index summary is followed by a list of archived and published references.

Folklorists eventually tracked down precursors of horror ULs in earlier writings. In 1945, when Baughman first published an oral version of "The Cadaver Arm" in *Hoosier Folklore Bulletin,* he mentioned that another account, included in Bennett Cerf 's column in a recent issue of *Saturday Review of Literature,* was "the only printed version I know." Since then, however, many other versions of the story have been collected as well as identified in early published literature, including this example from the Spanish author Pío Baroja in his novel *The Tree of Knowledge,* first published in English in 1928:

> There was a story of a second-year student who had played the following prank on a friend who, he knew, was rather timid. He took a dead man's arm, wrapped it in his cloak and went up to greet his friend.
>
> "How do you do?" he said, putting out the hand of the corpse from beneath his cloak.

"Well, and you?"—answered the other and shook his hand but shuddered at the coldness of it—and was horrified when he saw the arm of a dead man coming out from the cloak.

An even older literary version was written by the Danish author Jorgen Wilhelm Bergsoe, first translated in 1909 as "The Amputated Arm," and there are doubtless more early prototypes.

Compare the mere plot outline of "The Cadaver Arm" in the folklorist's index or the literary retellings of the story with the two oral versions given under the "Dangerous Pranks and Fatal Initiations" heading in this chapter. Even these transcribed spoken texts may seem somewhat dry on the printed page, yet people who have heard such stories told by skilled narrators in spooky settings often report feelings like "It just gives me the willies." Author Jayne Anne Phillips captures the storytelling context and the audience reaction nicely in her fictional treatment of "The Hook," titled "Blind Girls," also quoted below. A parody of "The Hook" is also included to suggest how adolescents eventually grow out of these teenage scares.

The horror legends that high school and undergraduate students were discovered to be hooked on reflect a worldview punctuated by grisly accounts of threats and attacks against people of their same age—most often females. Danger lurks everywhere, threatening them even when they were engaged in such pedestrian activities as babysitting, driving, shopping, socializing, and attending college. These stories came to be recognized as the classic examples of the horror UL genre, establishing the structure and style of later horror legends. As more such stories were collected and studied, it became obvious that they belonged to an international genre of modern oral narratives and had innumerable variations of detail and style. I have included another version of "The Roommate's Death," a legend already told in the introduction, just to show how differently the same story may be presented by different tellers. For a dramatized version of "The Babysitter and the Man Upstairs," rendered as a radio play, complete with sound effects, check out the CD/audiotape made by a storytelling group at Hanford High School, in California, that calls itself "Voices of Illusion." Their performances can be accessed via the Web site www.youthstorytelling.com, under the section for Kevin Cordi, the students' teacher and adviser. As I wrote in a cover blurb for the production, "These hip California high school students give a new imaginative twist to some old familiar Urban Legends."

The subjects of the classic horror ULs range from accounts of preteen rituals ("Bloody Mary"), through the stages of dating, driving, and entering college, and right up to medical school capers. Their power to haunt us, even in later years, when we "know better," is strengthened by their being told as the "actual" experiences of the ubiquitous friend of a friend, as well as by the plots' similarities to horror films and to genuine news stories about the actions of actual criminals and terrorists. As I was starting to write this book a story appeared in the October 13, 2002, issue of the *Pittsburgh Post-Gazette* headlined "Woman Fends Off Attacker with Kick, Pepper Spray, Car." Guess what? The attacker was lurking under her parked car just like the slasher of the well-known legend. But we must be careful not to conclude from such incidents that the story is not a legend after all. Remember, the slasher legend came first, and it was told in countless variations. The Pittsburgh case sounds like a copycat crime, or it may have been just a coincidence.

Over and over again newspapers investigate rumor and legend scares that sweep through the community without finding a trace of evidence to confirm them. I mention just three examples of such news items referring to hairy-armed hitchhikers and ankle slashers from the 1980s, giving the headlines alone:

> "Cutting Apart Ax Man Myth," *St. Louis Post-Dispatch*, June 1, 1983
> "Police Debunk 'Little Old Lady' Tale of Terror," *Fresno Bee*, April 30, 1983
> "Mall Slasher, in Fact, Is Rumor Only," *Baltimore Evening Sun*, December 18, 1989

Just when you think these older horror ULs may have been laid to rest for good, another round of scary reports surfaces. In December 1992 the *Winston-Salem Journal* headlined a story "Rumors of Slashers at Mall Disputed," with a sidebar noting, "Nobody can find victims of 'robbers' who 'hide' under cars." The articles mentioned "dozens of reports in recent weeks of . . . mythical accounts of bizarre crimes." After the panic died down in North Carolina, a similar scare popped up in Louisiana, as the *Baton Rouge Advocate* noted in February 1993: "Tale of ax man is varied, but just a rumor." Here the classic account of a killer with an ax lurking in the backseat of a woman's car had acquired the typical contemporary motif of the man's confession that "he wants to be in a street gang and [this was] part of his initiation." After the police investigated the stories and judged them to be false, some citizens refused to believe. A Louisiana city's police chief is quoted as saying, "I had a lady argue with me until she was blue in the face. . . . She swore to me the police were lying."

I don't believe we've heard the last of the ax man, whose saga continues to be retold. The big mystery is why such stories lie dormant for years and then suddenly come to life once more.

One factor that allows horror ULs to keep on sending chills

up our spines is that people sometimes hear the old stories for the first time as told (or e-mailed) by a trusted relative or friend. The plots, though bizarre and unlikely, are full of the prosaic details of everyday life, and good old so-and-so wouldn't lie, would he (or she)? The crime stories often return just before Christmas, when mall traffic is heavy and the disparity between happy holidays and violent attacks provides a dramatic contrast. Another factor in the legends' favor is that the details keep changing, while the basic patterns stay the same. The warnings always sound new, serious, and specific. Nowadays, for example, the mall-attack stories tend to mention a particular home-town setting and to describe not a clichéd ax-wielding stalker but rather a phony perfume salesman, or a man who claims to be recruiting people for a television commercial, or a helpful stranger offering to change a woman's flat tire. In another trans-formation, two older stories such as "The Killer in the Backseat" and "The Slasher under the Car" are combined into a warning about a "new" kind of crime, often associated with gang initia-tions. Sometimes details in the legends multiply, so that instead of simply a meat cleaver or an ax, the assailant has stockpiled "a gun, hunting knife, duct tape, rope, a gallon jug of sugar water, and two pairs of women's underwear!!!!!!!!!" (See Chapter 9 for all of these newer examples, and for an explanation of what the sugar water is for.)

Maybe adults have outgrown most of the babysitting, park-ing, and campus legends (although some of today's kids still tell them, more or less seriously), but we continue to have plenty of horror ULs, both revivals and new inventions, to share, either orally or electronically. A contemporary shocking event, such as the terrorist attacks of September 11, 2001, may enter the current urban legend repertoire, either supplementing or replacing the earlier meaning of 911 (as in emergency tele-phone calls) mentioned in classic stories such as "The Baby-sitter and the Man Upstairs."

In an e-mail I received recently, a fellow folklorist commented, "I can't keep up with Internet legendry; whatever became of oral tradition?" As the stories in this and the following chapters illustrate, we still have plenty of legends going around, some through the oral tradition and even more through electronic media.

"Bloody Mary"

One urban legend still haunts me from my childhood: "Bloody Mary." The version I know is, if someone went into the bathroom, shut off the light, and looked into the mirror and said "Bloody Mary" three times, a woman would appear in the mirror covered in blood. I can't remember for what reason, but she would either scratch your face or kill you. I know it sounds crazy, but in my childhood memories I actually remember a girl who was supposed to have done this and came out of the bathroom with deep scratches on her face.

• • •

I have a vivid memory of telling my friend about "Bloody Mary." One faced a mirror in a closed, darkened room—we used the bathroom—closed your eyes, and repeated "Bloody Mary" fifty times. When you opened your eyes, she would be in the mirror. I don't know if it works, since we chickened out at forty-nine. I heard the story from two girls who insisted they had seen Bloody Mary themselves. . . . I can tell you that I heard this when I was about nine years old, and to this day—

I am now twenty-six and my friend twenty-five—neither of us will keep an uncovered mirror in our bedroom. I am afraid to walk past a darkened room if it has a mirror visible from the doorway. Silly, I know, but it just gives me the willies.

• • •

*D*uring recess at school, you go into the girls' bathroom. Your friends wait outside because only [one] person is allowed in at a time. One girl stands at the door to turn out the lights once you're positioned in front of the mirror. Once the lights are out, you close your eyes and turn around three times. Then you open them and stare straight into the mirror and chant, "Bloody Mary, show your fright. Show your fright this starry night." You have to chant slowly so she has time to come from the spirit world. Then you wait to see her face. Once you see her, you have to run out of the bathroom where your friends are waiting. If you've sinned or done anything evil in your life then you will have three scratches of blood on your cheek.

The first version was sent to me by Lee Koechig of Phoenix, Arizona, in 1998; the second came from Susan M. Trevaskis of Cerritos, California, in 1990. The third is from Alan Dundes, "Bloody Mary in the Mirror: A Ritual Reflection of Pre-Pubescent Anxiety," Western Folklore *57 (1998): p. 123, where it is quoted from the University of California, Berkeley, student folklore archive. This version was shared among students in the third grade in 1983 at an elementary school in Louisiana.*

"The Babysitter and the Man Upstairs"

Babysitter's Nightmare Becomes Real!
It sounds like a headline in a supermarket tabloid, but actually it was an advertising slogan for *When a Stranger Calls*,

a 1979 thriller that still shows up now and then on pay-TV and the late, late, late movie.

Ads for the film featured a close-up photo of a terrified teenage girl, staring wide-eyed at a telephone. This doubtless was meant to remind people of the horror legend on which the film is based, the one folklorists call "The Babysitter and the Man Upstairs," a favorite among teenagers, especially babysitters. The film opens with a chilling dramatization of the legend; in fact, it's one of the scariest enactments of a horror UL that I know of, and worth staying up for:

A teenage girl is babysitting for the first time in a large, expensive house. She puts the children to bed upstairs and has just sat down in front of the TV when the telephone rings.

Judging by the voice, the caller is a man. He breathes heavily into the receiver, cackles menacingly, and asks, "Have you checked the children?"

The babysitter hangs up, thinking her friends are playing a prank on her.

But the man calls back, asking again, "Have you checked the children?" She quickly hangs up, but right away he calls a third time, this time saying, "I've already got the children, and now I'm going to get *you*!"

Now the babysitter is really alarmed. She calls the police and describes the threatening calls. They tell her that if he calls back, she should keep him on the line, so they can trace the call.

Sure enough, a few minutes later the man calls again. The babysitter pleads with him to leave her alone, thus detaining him. Finally he hangs up.

Suddenly the phone rings again, and with every call the telephone bell seems to get louder and more insistent. But this time it is the police calling with the urgent command, "Get out of the house right away! Those calls are coming from an upstairs extension!"

Usually the legend simply ends there, leaving it to the listener to imagine what might happen next. Sometimes it is said that when the police arrive and search the house, they find the children murdered and the killer lurking on the stairway with a knife. The filmmakers, however, continued the story right on through the caller's capture, his prison term, his eventual release, and the continuation of the babysitter's nightmare as he stalks her. Frankly, these additions are not as scary as the opening, so it's OK to change the channel or go to bed after watching just the first part of *When a Stranger Calls*.

Adapted from my newspaper column "Urban Legends," where it was released for publication the week of December 28, 1987, under the title "A Sitter's Frightening House Call."

"The Hook"

We were sitting around and it was like about 12 o'clock at midnight at a slumber party about two years ago. [And someone told this story.]

Once there was a couple and they were dating and they went out to a [laughs because she is inhibited by the tape recorder and me] they were out in the middle of the woods by a lake parking. And they were making out and they had their radio on. There came a flash on the radio to beware that on the outskirts of the town there was a man with a hook on his hand who had escaped from a prison and to beware because if they saw anybody with a hook hand that he was dangerous. And so they sat there for a while, you know, and the girl started getting scared. She looked over and she locked her door and he locked his door and he said, "This is really ridiculous getting upset about it." And she said, "Well, you know, I'm kinda scared about this thing." So they sat there for a while and she said, "Listen, let's go into town." And he said, "No, no let's don't worry about it, don't worry about it." And she said, "Listen, I'm getting kinda scared, well, let's go into town." And so he goes, "OK." So he takes, he takes her into town and when they drive up to her house, he gets out and he goes over to the side of the door and on the door was a hook.

AUDIENCE: [low laughter]

MISSY: That went over great. [sarcastic tone]

· · ·

She knew it was only boys in the field, come to watch them drunk on first wine. A radio in the little shack poured out promises of black love and lips. Jesse watched Sally paint her hair with grenadine, dotting the sticky syrup on her arms. The party was in a shack down the hill from her house, beside a field of tall grass where black snakes lay like flat belts. The Ripple bottles were empty and Jesse told pornographic stories about various adults while everyone laughed; about Miss Hicks the home-ec teacher whose hands were dimpled and moist and always touching them. It got darker and the stories got scarier. Finally she told their favorite, the one about the girl and her boyfriend parked on a country road on a night like this, with the wind blowing and then rain, the whole sky sobbing potato juice. Please let's leave, pleads girlie, It sounds like something scratching at the car. For God's sake, grumbles boyfriend, and takes off squealing. At home they find the hook of a crazed amputee caught in the door. Jesse described his yellow face, putrid, and his blotchy stump. She described him panting in the grass, crying and looking for something. She could feel him smelling of raw vegetables, a rejected bleeding cowboy with wheat hair, and she was unfocused. Moaning in the dark and falsetto voices. Don't don't please don't. Nervous laughter. Sally looked out the window of the shack. The grass is moving, she said, Something's crawling in it. No, it's nothing. Yes, there's something coming, and her voice went up at the end. It's just boys trying to scare us. But Sally whined and flailed her arms. On her knees she hugged Jesse's legs and mumbled into her thighs. It's all right, I'll take you up to the house. Sally was stiff, her nails digging the skin. She wouldn't move. Jesse tied a scarf around her eyes and led her like a horse through fire up the hill to the house, one poison light soft in a window. Boys ran out of the field squawling.

• • •

Once there was a man whose right arm had been blown off at the elbow in the war. He had to wear a hook, but it didn't bother him in his job. He worked the night shift at the 7-11, and he had learned to operate the cash register with his left hand.

One dark night as he was walking home from work on a dirt road sometimes used as a Lover's Lane, something very strange happened. As he hurried past a black clump of trees, he felt something catch on his hook and give it a hard tug. He took off running as fast as he could, but he couldn't escape the feeling that something was pulling on his hook. He still felt it as he jumped into bed and covered his head.

His first thought when he awoke the next morning was that it was just a bad dream. Then he looked down at his hook hanging off the side of his bed.

Attached to it was a small sports car containing two horrified teenagers.

The first version was told by Missy Hudson, then a nineteen-year-old college student, when she recorded "The Hook" before an audience of fellow students for folklorist Danielle Roemer, who published this text in "Scary Story Legends," Folklore Annual *3 (1971): pp. 1–16 (the first brack-*

eted comment is mine; the rest are Roemer's). The second version is Jayne Anne Phillips's story "Blind Girls," from Philips's book Black Tickets *(New York: Delacorte Press, 1979). The parody of "The Hook" is by Ron Coulthard and appeared under the title "Hooked" in* Cold Mountain Review, *published by Appalachian State University, Boone, North Carolina, in 1985.*

"Severed Fingers"

In 1954ish there was a popular small car, the Renault Dauphine. Engine at the back with an air grill. Bloke from the BBC working late finally departs for home at 2 A.M. in his Dauphine. In Soho he's stopped at traffic lights, when a group of Teddy Boys surround his car and start bouncing it. Not waiting for a green light, he shoves the car into first gear, revs up and off, in a sudden burst of speed. At home, shutting the garage doors, he notices two severed fingers stuck in the rear engine air grill. Next morning 'round to the local police station to report the whole incident. "Not to worry," says the sergeant. "We'll put these in the lost property and if they are claimed we'll know who the villains are."

•   •   •

A commercial traveler with whom I did business was returning home through Leicester late in the evening and was halted at a red traffic light. Four youths who had been loitering on the corner moved over to him and grasping bumpers, wings, etc. began to rock his Volkswagen Beetle; the movement quickly becoming more violent. As the crossing traffic was fairly heavy, the driver could not move off, so he put his car in first gear, revved the engine, and when the light changed shot off like a bomb. Next morning he found four fingers jammed in the ventilating slits in the rear of the car.

• • •

Mrs. Campbell remembered residing in an Old Town house, which was one night disturbed in the most intolerable manner by a drunken party at the knocker. In the morning the greater part of it was found to be gone; and it was besides discovered to the horror of the inmates, that part of a finger was left sticking in the fragments, with the appearance of having been forcibly wrenched from the hand.

The first and second versions were sent to me by English readers in 1985 and 1982, respectively. The third version is a precursor of the story discovered by folklorist Sandy Hobbs in Chambers's Traditions of Edinburgh, *first published in 1824; Hobbs re-published it in his article "The Folk Tale as News,"* Oral History 6 (1978): p. 75.

"The Boyfriend's Death"

A guy and his girlfriend are on the way to a party when their car starts to give them some trouble. At that same time they catch a news flash on the radio warning all people in the area that a lunatic killer has escaped from a local criminal asylum. The girl becomes very upset and at that point the car stalls completely on the highway. The boyfriend gets out and tinkers around with the engine but can't get the car to start again. He decides that he is going to have to walk on up the road to a gas station and get a tow truck but wants his girlfriend to stay behind in the car. She is frightened and pleads with him to take her, but he says that she'll be safe on the floor of the car covered with a blanket so that anyone passing will think it is an abandoned car and not bother her. Besides he can sprint along the road and get back more quickly than if she comes with him in her high-heeled shoes and evening dress. She finally agrees and he tells her not to come out unless she hears his signal of three knocks on the window, kisses her goodbye, tucks her under the cover, locks the door, and sprints off down the road.

A half hour or so goes by although it seems like years to the girl. Suddenly she hears a knock and is about to get up when she remembers her boyfriend's warning of waiting for three knocks. She waits, and hears two, three, four, five, six, seven, and they continue! She remains motionless and it just continues. Finally it stops and she hears voices outside. She peeks out and the policemen are crowded around the car and call to her to come out, that it's all right. She opens a door, comes out, and the police lead her to one of their cars, cautioning her not to look back. Despite this she turns and sees her boyfriend hung from the limb of a tree above the car and his feet are barely touching the roof—that was the continuous knocking sound!

● ● ●

I heard this whilst living in West Germany in 1974 or 1975.

A young couple were driving through a forest in Denmark along a little-used road when, without warning, the car stopped. The boyfriend diagnosed the problem as lack of fuel, got out his empty jerry can, and set out to walk the few kilometres to the nearest village. He left strict instructions with the girl to lock herself in the car and not to get out under any circumstances.

She waited for a long while, but there was no sign of her boyfriend returning. Then she heard a "tap, tap, tap" noise on the car roof. She remembered what her boyfriend had said, and stayed in the car with the doors locked. All the while the tapping went on, and she became more and more terrified.

Finally, another car came along, but it merely slowed down, and then sped away. Shortly after that, two police cars arrived, and through a loudspeaker she heard the police telling her to leave the car, walk over to them, and not to look back.

She got out and walked over to the police cars, but just as she got there she looked back at her own car, and there she saw—hanging from the tree above the car—a madman, tapping on the roof of the car with her boyfriend's severed head!

The first version is from Susan Smith's collection "Urban Tales," in Edith Fowke's Folklore of Canada *(Toronto: McClelland and Stewart, 1976), pp. 263–64; I quoted part of this text, told by a fourteen-year-old male, in* The Vanishing Hitchhiker, *pp. 8–9. The second version was sent to me in 1980 by Ken Lussey of Lincoln, England.*

"The Killer in the Backseat"

I heard this from a friend who swears it is true.

A woman drove into the Standard gas station on Pacific Coast Highway (our neighborhood) in Malibu and asked for a fill-up. The station attendant obliged, then walked to her driver's-window side and asked for $19.63 in payment. When she handed him a $20.00 bill from her wallet he studied the bill—looking carefully at it, then pulling another from his pocket and comparing the two. He then said to the woman, "This is a counterfeit, a phony, lady—you will have to come with me. The rules are that I must inform my boss and he will call the bank and then you will need to give him the information on your bank and where you might have picked up this bill."

The woman protested that she was in a hurry and knew nothing of the origin of the bill, etc. The attendant opened her car door and coaxed the woman from the car, even taking her by the hand. The woman, protesting any knowledge of such things, did allow herself to be guided into the little station-office enclosure.

There the attendant dialed the sheriff's number and turned his ashen face to her saying, "Madam, there is no problem with your money; however, there is a crazy looking man crouching in the back of your car, clutching a hatchet!"

• • •

Police Officer Says
Common Sense May Prevent Assault

PHOENIX (UPI)—As the woman walked to her car in a parking lot, she noticed a man following her.

She jumped in her car and tore off, only to notice to her dismay that the man was following her in his car.

The woman drove through downtown Phoenix trying to elude him, passing stores, houses and bars. When that failed, she drove across town to the home of her brother-in-law, a policeman.

Horn honking, she pulled up and her brother-in-law came running out. She explained a man was following her and "There he is, right there!"

The policeman ran up to the man's car and demanded to know what he was doing.

"Take it easy. All I wanted to do was tell her about the guy in her back seat." The man said.

And indeed, there was a man huddled in the woman's back seat.

This true incident of several years ago is an example used by Lt. [name deleted], public information officer and head of the Phoenix police department's community services department.

He relates the tale to show the importance for women in locking their car doors and keeping car windows closed. . . .

A big, attractive man in his 40's, [the lieutenant] does his best to keep the audience awake with humorous and somewhat graphic stories. . . .

Public Service Notice

Female residents may want to exercise extra caution when getting gas for their cars at gas stations. Here's why:

Recently at the Juanita BP gas station, (98 N.E. and Juanita Drive N.E.), a man slipped into a woman's car, unseen by her as she returned from prepaying her gas at the deli/gas store.

Fortunately for her, the attendant, who is usually quite busy at his counter, just happened to notice a young Asian male entering the back door of her car. He quickly dialed 911 and while she was pumping the gas, he accused her tactfully three times of not paying for her gas—to get her to come back into the store. Rather than getting back into her car, she came steaming into the store to let him know she HAD paid for the gas.

He quickly explained what had happened. When the Kirkland police arrived and arrested the intruder, they explained to her that part of the initiation process for membership in some Asian gangs is that the recruit must either Rape or 'Slash' a white woman. This man was apparently stalking this gas station to see what unsuspecting woman would leave her car unlocked, so he could carry out his mission.

That alert attendant was praised by the police in that he just may have saved that innocent woman's life. These recruits select and stalk neighborhoods—

like ours—where there is no gang activity and single-out women who are careless when they leave their cars at gas stations and convenience stores.

Please share this information with other women that you have contact with; it just might save their lives. Many women are now getting their gas at stations where one pays out where the gas pumps are, rather than having to walk some distance into a store to make the payment.

Why not be selective where you buy gas and lessen the chance for danger?

(This information has been brought to us by North End Taxi, who serves our area. 363-3333)

The first version was sent to me in 1982 by a woman in Malibu, California. The second is the beginning of a feature story published in the Flagstaff *(Arizona)* Sun, *on July 17, 1980, probably reprinted from a Phoenix newspaper. The "Public Service Notice" was taken from a bulletin board in the Seattle area around 1994.*

"The Hairy-Armed Hitchhiker"

I was told this story in 1978, and it had particular salience at the time because it was when the man known as the Yorkshire Ripper was at large. He had already raped, murdered, or attempted to murder several young women.

The story was that a young woman is going one evening to a meeting at a hospital. The meeting is something to do with her work and the hospital is some way out of town. She sets off driving along the dual carriageway, and it is very dark. She listens to the radio as she drives and hears yet another warning from the police that women should not be traveling alone at night while the Ripper is still at large.

The young woman sees an older woman walking along the road, and she stops, offering her a lift, which she gratefully accepts. The older woman gets in the car, and the two continue their journey. As the two women talk, the young woman notices that the older woman's hands are very hairy— more like a man's hands, in fact. She becomes so anxious she works out a plan to get the older woman out of the car.

She puts her car headlights on full beam so that they are dazzling all the cars coming in the opposite direction. The other cars flash her in annoyance, and she points out to the older woman that there must be something wrong with her car since all the others are flashing her.

So she asks the older woman to get out to look at the lights while she adjusts them, tries them out, etc. The older woman gets out of the car to check, and the young woman drives off, relieved to have got rid of her passenger. She goes to her meeting, thinking no more of the incident, but when she gets back into her car again, she notices that the old woman had left her bag in it. She opens the bag to discover a hefty meat cleaver, and she hurries to the police with it.

• • •

I am attending the Los Angeles School of Broadcasters. Last night I had a class called Commercial Interpretation. Each student was assigned a commercial to practice over the next few days. Mine was for the Sherman Oaks Galleria, a shopping mall in Sherman Oaks, California, with "plenty of free parking." This morning, I practiced it on my friend Laurie.

Before I got any farther than "You can shop in style at the new Sherman Oaks Galleria," she interrupted.

"Ooh, the Galleria! Did I tell you what happened to a friend of Janet's [a mutual friend] at the mall last year?"

"No, you didn't," I said.

"Well, it was Christmastime, see, and she was taking a bunch of packages out to her car. She opened the door—and there was this little old lady sitting in the backseat! Janet's friend asked her what she was doing there, and the old lady said, 'Oh, I'm sorry, but I was so cold and tired I broke into your car to get warm.' Janet's friend said, 'Oh, okay, you can stay here 'til I finish my shopping.' Then she put her packages in the trunk and went back into the store. But instead of finishing her shopping, she got a security guard, who went back out to the car with her. They found out that the 'old lady' was really a man dressed up as a woman—and guess what he was hiding under his dress?"

"Um," I said, "you tell me."

"An AX!!"

(I suspected as much.)

The first version is typical of many sent to me by English readers in the early 1980s. The second account was sent to me by Christine Lehman on September 29, 1989; I substituted pseudonyms for the names of her informant and the mutual friend.

"The Slasher under the Car"

Our niece stopped by last night returning from a wedding in Rockford, Illinois. When coming around Chicago, they often stop at a large shopping mall in Merrillville, east of Chicago. One of her friends told her that she had better *not* stop there this time as she had heard this story about it.

There has been a man there hiding under women's cars, and when they come close to the car to unlock it, he reaches out with a knife or razor and slashes their ankles. Then as they reach their hands down to their ankles, he grabs their hands, pulls them down, and robs them.

* * *

I heard this two Christmases ago from our office manager. He had the misfortune to get a traffic ticket, and in order to avoid collecting the dreaded "points" on his license, he was required to attend a traffic safety course. The following story was told by the officer giving the course during the "crime prevention" segment.

"There is a sadistic killer roaming the Southwest who is preying on women shoppers during the Christmas season. His modus operandi is to hide under the victim's car until she returns laden with packages. As she struggles to unlock her car door without dropping anything, he suddenly lashes out from beneath the car with a tire iron, breaking both her ankles. The pain is so sudden and intense that the victim is unable to make a sound, and she falls to the ground. The killer then quickly bundles her into her own car and spirits her away to a secluded spot, where she is tortured and killed. This killer recently abducted a woman from a shopping center here in Phoenix, and her body was found in the desert with multiple one-inch squares of skin sliced away. She had died from loss of blood."

When someone in the class asked why such a gruesome murder had not been covered by the local press, the officer smiled knowingly and replied, "Plenty of things like that never get into the papers."

The first version was sent to me by Mrs. Russell Lee of Fort Wayne, Indiana, in September 1984; the second came from Dr. Charles Gauntt of Phoenix, Arizona, in July 1986.

"Dangerous Pranks and Fatal Initiations"

"The Fatal Fraternity Initiation"

Charlie, my older brother, told me this story several years ago before he went into the army. At that time, I doubted the validity of the tale. Now, after studying psychology and psychological effects on a person, I am inclined to believe it could have happened.

There was a death in one of the fraternity houses of a large eastern university. It was a most peculiar situation. Here is how it happened.

It was "Hell Week," and the active members were pulling their usual initiation stunts. All the pledges were right guys and were taking the ribbing and paddlings without any kick. Joe, a big, tough end on the football team, was doing all right too. As a matter of fact, he was almost too good and wasn't getting his share of the paddle. This didn't please the actives; so they concocted a scheme which they thought would even up Joe's score.

Early one evening four of the members escorted Joe into an automobile, just for a little joy ride. Joe must have known something was going to happen, because everyone was unusually quiet. They had planned a neat trick and everyone was curious about his reactions. Finally the car stopped at an old deserted farmhouse. They all looked at Joe.

"This is it," said the driver.

"Blindfold and gag him," came the instructions. "OK, now get him in the house." The others obeyed without a word.

Inside it was already dark, and they had to use flashlights. They made their way into the damp, cool cellar. The room had a brick floor and resounded loudly to their heavy shoes.

"All right," mumbled the leader, "stretch him out on that table." Again no answer came from the others. "Tie him down. Be sure to leave the left arm over the edge of the table." They obeyed. "Now, bring the knife and pan."

They placed the pan under Joe's left arm. The leader took hold of Joe's hand. Then he said, "This won't hurt, Joe. We just want to see if you can really take it. I'm just going to sliver the skin at the wrist and take a few drops of blood." Joe tried to get up, but the ropes were well tied. He couldn't yell because of the gag in his mouth. He lay there.

The leader ran the cool back-edge of the knife lightly over Joe's wrist. The other boys sighed as if something had really happened. Then one of them dripped water on the wrist, while another started water dripping in the pan from an especially constructed device. The set-up was perfect—"blood" dripping from Joe's wrist and falling in the pan.

"Well, Joe," said one of the actives, "we'll be back in several hours. Don't bleed too much." They left laughing.

A few hours later the four boys returned. They were still laughing and joking. They stopped at the basement stairway and listened. There was still the constant dripping of the "blood." "Joe's still there. He hasn't got away," they were thinking to themselves. So on down they went.

The boys flashed their lights on the table where Joe was lying. They walked over to him. He didn't make a sound and they thought he had fallen asleep. One of the boys removed the blindfold. Joe didn't open his eyes. Joe was dead!

"The Mock Execution"

A group of Birmingham students were discussing the question of hypnosis. They decided to try an experiment and invited into the lecture room a laboratory assistant who was always causing them problems and getting them into trouble.

They explained to him that no one could be made to do anything under hypnosis that they would not do when fully awake. They said that a student had been hypnotised, told to execute someone and they wanted the laboratory assistant to help them prove the student would not go through with it.

They asked the assistant to kneel down with his head bent as if ready to have his head chopped off. The "hypnotised" student was then brought in and with a suitable build-up he gently dropped a wet towel across the back of the victim's neck. Unfortunately, the assistant was of a nervous disposition and the shock brought on a heart attack which killed him.

"The Cadaver's Hand"

When I was in grade school, I was told this by a teacher—that at I.U. these nurses, living in the dorm, thought they'd be "real funny" to this one girl because nothing ever bothered her when they would work on the cadavers—never "fazed" her at all. So they decided they'd put this arm—well, it was a hand, more or less—a hand and wrist—hang it on the string they'd pull to turn on the light in the closet. So they went out that night, and she wasn't going out and they locked the door on her. They never heard anything and they didn't think too much about it—you know—thought, well, she was mad and just wouldn't let them back in the room. The next morning, she didn't come down and they didn't hear anything, so they got somebody to open the door. There she was in the closet; her hair was snow white and she was dead—of fright, supposedly.

"The Pickled Arm"

When I was a schoolgirl in Bellingham, Washington, I knew two sisters whose older brother was a doctor. He told them a story which he said he was sure was told to all young students in every medical college in America, "The Pickled Arm."

When young women first wished to become doctors

everyone knew no woman could be a good doctor and they must be discouraged. So, in a medical college, probably back east, or in the next state, there came a girl to study. The young men thought of various ways to force her to leave; one had to do with her finding a large dead frog in her soup. She picked it up and put it on the table and went on eating. Then there was a live angleworm in the baked beans. She picked it up and deposited it outdoors and went on calmly eating.

Then they had the perfect solution. When she was in a class they went to where they had various pickled parts of bodies and took a pickled arm and put it in her bed; then they waited for her screaming. She went upstairs to her room and soon . . . here she came slowly down the stairs, chewing the pickled arm. She had gone insane!

Years later I was working in an office in Portland, and one of the girls came back from lunch—she had met her mother, but neither could eat a thing. Her mother told her a horrible story, and it was true. A woman at the hairdresser told her . . . then I realized it was going to be the pickled arm story. When she was near the end of the story, I began to laugh. She was indignant. It was *true*! The woman who told her mother had a daughter whose best friend was a niece of a nurse at the insane asylum where the victim now was and often she would not go to bed but sat on the edge of her bed chewing her own arm.

"Joke Turns into Horror Story"

MEMPHIS, Tenn. (UPI)—The group that gathered in Forest Park Cemetery on soft summer nights enjoyed the goose-bumps that ghost stories beside a gravestone bring and the thrill of fear from strange noises in the night.

But when death itself showed up for the "grand finale," the screams no longer ended in giggles.

The group—ranging in age from 16 to 36, blacks and

whites, men and women—was in the habit of going to the graveyard for scary thrills, said police Capt. Larry Nevil, and last Friday they had some new initiates.

As a couple of old hands led the initiates to a pre-selected gravestone, others leaped out from behind trees and tombstones to frighten them. Once at the stone, they exchanged ghost stories.

On the way out, Nevil said, they were to encounter the "grand finale"—a man hanged from a tree.

One of those in the know, Stephen Shane Houston, 28, was keeping contact with the "hanged man" by a pre-arranged whistle signal and he got the last one "a matter of minutes" before they found his body swinging from the tree.

It scared them. Then, when the body continued to swing instead of jump down, it annoyed them.

"When he didn't get down, at first they thought he was kidding," said Nevil. "After a while it dawned on them he wasn't breathing."

Michael J. Kirsh, a computer sciences student at Memphis State University, died five days short of his 26th birthday, hanged by the neck.

Kirsch evidently miscalculated the length of his safety rope, which was attached to a harness around his chest. He made it longer than the rope with the hangman's knot around his neck.

The first story is from Ernest Baughman, "The Fatal Initiation," Hoosier Folklore Bulletin 4, no. 3 (September 1945): pp. 51–52. "The Mock Execution" is from Paul Smith, The Book of Nastier Legends (London: Routledge and Kegan Paul, 1986), p. 50; Smith also has a British version of "The Cadaver's Hand," on p. 79, which involves a human foot instead of a hand. "The Cadaver's Hand" is from of JoAnn Stephens Parochetti, "Scary Stories from Purdue," Keystone Folklore Quarterly 10 (1965): p. 53, as told by a Purdue University female student in 1963. "The Pickled Arm" was sent to me in 1989 by Ann Cary of Seattle, Washington, and was paraphrased in The Baby Train, *p. 315, as "Lending a Hand at Medical School." Edward Grogan of Indianapolis sent me the news story datelined Memphis, Tennessee, in January 1983; he remembered clipping it during the preceding autumn but did not record the source or date. This report describes a "legend trip" turned tragic.*

"The Roommate's Death"

There were these two girls, and they were roommates, and they went to a University, a small school and one night their school was having an all school campus dance and so the two girls decided to go to the dance and they thought they'd meet some boys that way, so when they got to the dance they were dancing and having a good time and then one of the girls got sick so she decided to go back to the dorm, she felt bad. But to get to the dorm from where the dance was, she had to go thru a woods, and there was a rumor out that a man had just escaped from an insane asylum and she was a little bit afraid to go back by herself, but she felt so bad and she didn't want her roommate to miss out on the fun so she told her she was going and she went ahead anyway.

So, on her way thru the woods she heard this heavy breathing sound coming up behind her and so she didn't want to turn back 'cause he was afraid because *she* was afraid she'd let them know that she had heard them, who was back there, so she walked a little bit faster and the panting got a little bit heavier behind her and she wasn't going to turn back and so she began to run, and so she ran all the way back to her dorm, but all the time she ran you could still hear the heavy panting behind her, and so she ran in the dorm and up the stairs and down the hallway and up to her room and she still heard the panting coming up behind her so she got in her room and she watched and the door knob began to turn.

So she got in the closet, because that was the only place she knew of that she could get in and she heard the door of her room open and so while she was in the closet there began this scraping on the outside of her closet door. Scrape, scrape, scrape, like the sound of claws and this heavy breathing and panting, and the girl screamed until a counselor who was on duty heard her scream and when the counselor came upstairs, she found the girl's roommate outside the closet door with her throat slit. She had been afraid her roommate would come in contact with the man from the insane asylum and she had followed her all the way back to the dorm and had had her own throat slit.

Version B, told by an Indiana University student in 1967, from Linda Dégh, "The Roommate's Death and Related Dormitory Stories in Formation," Indiana Folklore 2 *(1969): pp. 56–57.*

"The Curse of 9/11"

An e-mail dated 1/12/02:

Yesterday I had a very peculiar experience that I told to a few friends via e-mail last night. I consider what happened to be a near astronomical coincidence, and I imagine people could read all sorts of things into it. It could possibly turn into a full blown UL. Here's my report as I e-mailed it:

So I get a call today from an old client. He wants me to come uptown [in New York City] to fix a system we put up back in the mid '90s . . . a big video wall display in the window of the American Bible Society on Broadway at 60th street. The system has been dead for weeks; something's corrupted the video wall software.

It's an old computer running DOS. I take a quick look on the hard drive and find that all of the key files needed to run the video wall are missing. Running diagnostic software tells me there's a big chunk of corrupted data on the disk.

"I have no idea what would have done that" I say. "It's an old computer and we haven't looked at it for a few years. You say the problem developed over the holidays?"

The client nodded his head.

"Maybe you got a delayed Y2K problem around new years." I said. "Let's take a look at the system clock."

I typed in TIME.

The machine read 08:46:00

"That's not right. It's just past 3:30 pm," I said, glancing at my watch. "Let's see what day it thinks it is."

I typed in DATE.

The machine read 09:11:01.

[Insert spooky music here.]

• • •

An e-mail forwarded to me on 11/22/01:

ORIGINAL LETTER:

The date of the attack: 9/11—9 + 1 + 1 = 11

September 11th is the 254th day of the year: 2 + 5 + 4 = 11.

After September 11th there are 111 days left to the end of the year.

119 is the area code to Iraq/Iran. 1 + 1 + 9 = 11

The Twin Towers, standing side by side, looks like the number 11

The first plane to hit the towers was Flight 11.

State of New york — the 11th state added to the union.

New York City — 11 letters.

Afghanistan — 11 letters.

The Pentagon — 11 letters.

Ramzi Yousef — 11 letters (convicted of orchestrating the attack on the WTC in 1993)

Flight 11 — 92 on board – 9 + 2 = 11

Flight 77 — 65 on board – 6 + 5 = 11

DAVE'S RESPONSE:

Oh my God! How worried should I be? There are 11 letters in my name, "David _ _ _ _ _!" I'm going into hiding NOW. See you in a few weeks.

Wait a sec . . . just realized "YOU CAN'T HIDE" also has 11 letters! What am I gonna do? Help me!!! The terrorists are after me! ME! I can't believe it! Oh crap, there must be someplace on the planet Earth I could hide! But no . . . "PLANET EARTH" has 11 letters, too!

Maybe Nostradamus can help me. But dare I trust him" there are 11 letters in "NOSTRADAMUS." I know, the Red Cross can help. No they can't . . . 11 letters in "THE RED CROSS," can't trust them. I would rely on self defense, but "SELF DEFENSE" has 11 letters in it too! Can someone help?

Anyone? If so, send me email. No, don't . . . "SEND ME EMAIL" has 11 letters.

Will this never end? I'm going insane! "GOING INSANE???" Eleven letters!!

Oh my God, I just realized that America is doomed! Our Independence Day is July 4th . . . 7/4 . . . 7 + 4 = 11!

Dave

PS. "ITS BULLSHIT" has 11 letters also.

These two examples demonstrate how the paranoia following the 9/11 terrorist attacks gave new meaning to the numbers involved and inspired both serious concerns and debunking parodies. The first example came from Jon Kiphart of Cold Spring, New York, whose "insert spooky music" comment indicates his skepticism. The second example was sent to me by folklorist Simon Carmel, who did not know the "Dave" named in it. I omitted the last name but want to point out that the name Jan Brunvand also has eleven letters!

IF A BODY MEETS A BODY

There are a lot of bodies in horror ULs; many are decayed or mutilated, and most are found in unexpected places. Corpses show up in trains, cars, hotel rooms, at border crossings, in packages or barrels, and—not surprisingly—in medical school anatomy labs, except that these last ones are the wrong bodies in the right place. No matter how you look at it, if you meet a body in an urban legend, it's chilling. And it's not merely the shock of stumbling upon a corpse; in a couple of these stories someone even accidentally *ingests* part of the dead body. Talk about a bad meal!

The stories in this chapter all have wide circulation and many variations, and so I have selected a few international texts and variant versions to suggest the broader tradition. Many other examples might be given. For instance, "Origin of Packenham's Rum" is just an American retelling of a common legend. The same "Corpse in the Cask" story is told about Admiral Horatio Nelson, whose body was shipped home in 1805; that particular incident supposedly spawned the expression "tapping the admiral," a reference to sailors drinking off the alcohol used to preserve a body at sea. A modern urban legend version of the same story describes an English family that inherits a large country house in the cellar of which they find several barrels of rum; only *after* the family has drunk most of the rum do they discover that one of the barrels holds the corpse of a man who had been shipped home from the colonies generations ago. The same theme of *cannibalisme involontaire* is so well known in France that an entire chapter in a recent book is devoted to discussing the legend of "Le cadavre dans la cuve" (The Cadaver in the Wine Vat). It's in Véronique Campion-Vincent and Jean-Bruno Renard's book *Legendes urbaines: Rumeurs d'aujourd'hui* (1992).

Sometimes we can go surprisingly far back in finding analogues for modern horror ULs. To all the contemporary stories about decapitated passengers or pets riding in motorcycles, cars, and trucks, we may compare this little gem reported from a stagecoach rider in Charles Dickens's *The Pickwick Papers*, published in the 1830s:

> "Heads, heads—take care of your heads!" cried the loquacious stranger, as they came out under the low archway, which in those days formed the entrance to the coach-yard. "Terrible place—dangerous work— other day—five children—mother—tall lady, eating sandwiches—forgot the arch—crash—knock—children look round—mother's head off—sandwich in her hand—no mouth to put it in—head of a family off—shocking, shocking!"

Some of these body horror stories come rather close to real life. The account of the British novelist Laurence Sterne's corpse being stolen from the grave and dissected by medical students (see "The Face Is Familiar") was repeated for many years as God's own truth but was finally debunked by recent historians. Then in the twentieth century, an actual relative's cadaver incident happened in an American university, as the letter I quote from a medical journal attests. This factual instance of a student's great aunt becoming an anatomy-lab subject, which differed somewhat from the "folk" stories, was altered further by the media into a somewhat more dramatic account, accompanied in *Esquire* (January 1984) by the quip "The white gloves gave her away" and in *Omni* (November 1982) by a staged photo of a female medical student gazing with horror at a draped cadaver. An analytic approach to such med-school tales was taken by Dr. Frederic W. Hafferty in his learned article "Cadaver Stories and the Emotional Socialization of Medical Students" (*Journal of Health and Social Behavior* 29 [December 1988]: pp. 344–56).

The "Lost Wreck" legend offers a good example of the difference between real-life horrors and folk versions. I have quoted the full 1985 newspaper report from Canada of a local legend that is loaded with evidence of its apocryphal nature. Besides the official denials by Officers Dumpleton and Rumple and other local officials, this news account of a regional horror story is clearly differentiated from the occasional factual reports of similar accidents by its variant versions, by the FOAF source, by the mention of a possible cover-up, and by the folkloristic motif of the victims' discovery being triggered by the sound of a thrown object hitting metal in a forest, a detail probably borrowed from an old Norwegian legend. A similar debunking could be done with the "Body on the Car" news stories that, unfortunately, occasionally do appear but, again, are different in detail from the stylized legend form. There are also various odd news items about bodies found in hotel rooms, in or near the bed, that might seem to validate (although I doubt it) the widely told "Body in the Bed" legend as literally true.

Speaking of claims of truth, no less respected sources than *Life, New Republic,* the *Washington Post,* and *National Geographic* have published versions of the "Stuffed Baby" legend as reports of an actual atrocity, even though drug enforcement authorities have repeatedly debunked it and no verifiable instance has come to light. It's possible that some drug smugglers may eventually copy the legend and act out its horror, but surely there must be safer, neater, and more reliable methods to bring drugs into a country illegally.

Certainly not "The Stuffed Baby" and perhaps not most other stories in this chapter, but *some* horror ULs are sometimes converted by storytellers into performances in such a way that they resemble jokes more than legends. I've heard performances of horror legends such as "The Corpse in the Cask" and "The Eaten Cremains" (included here as "The Mixup in the Mail") narrated for laughs rather than for shudders. After all, laughter—especially nervous laughter—seems to be a natural reaction to some kinds of horror. Chief Dumpleton, according to the news story, "chuckled when asked about the mystery" of "The Lost Wreck." And the woman who told me the "Body in the Bed" legend said that after her friends in the book club cross-examined the earnest storyteller who told it and she finally admitted she knew only about friends of friends as sources, they all "laughed loud and long."

"The Creepy Passenger"

A young woman visitor to Cape Town is very impressed by the local railway system. Her friends, however, are full of dark warnings "never to travel third class, especially at night when some weird things can happen."

One night, however, she is forced to take the train home from Kalk Bay and for some reason gets on a third class coach. These carriages, as you know, are arranged with long seats up against the sides and an aisle down the centre. The only other passengers in the coach are three fairly well-dressed young black men huddled together towards one end, and an older, rather wild-eyed black man sitting reading a newspaper at the opposite side of the carriage from the other group.

Only the old man looks up as the young woman enters the train and, alarmed by the intensity of his gaze, she naturally sits closer to the three men, diagonally across from them. The old man begins to slide along his seat towards her, still holding his paper in front of him.

She looks anxiously at the young men for support, but

they continue to stare straight ahead of them. The one in the centre appears to be drunk, as his head lolls from side to side with the movement of the train while he looks fixedly at a point opposite him.

The older man slowly traverses the entire length of the carriage until he is next to the now-frantic woman, and she can smell his booze-and-sweat odour as he leans towards her and asks in a low and croaky voice: "Have you read the news today?"

Too terrified to move, the woman takes the proffered newspaper and reads the scribbled note hidden inside. The note reads: GET OFF AT THE NEXT STOP. THE MAN IN THE MIDDLE IS DEAD.

From Arthur Goldstuck, The Aardvark and the Caravan: South Africa's Greatest Urban Legends *(London: Penguin Books, 1999), pp. 35–36. Often titled "The Man in the Middle," this UL is widely told in other countries, sometimes as an account of an undergraduate prank.*

"Origin of Packenham's Rum"

Along the Gulf Coast a particular kind of rum is called "Packenham." Helen Weaver of Tallahasee learned of its origin from her father:

"We hear a lot about General Jackson in this part of Florida around Tallahasee. Jackson was our commander at the Battle of New Orleans. The English commander was Packenham. My great-grandfather had a cousin, Henry Hunter, who was a soldier in that battle, and it is likely that he fired the shot that killed General Packenham.

"When my father was a boy of ten, old Henry was ninety and blind. He would sit for hours telling of fighting the

Indians and hunting for bear and deer. As you know from your history books, General Jackson's men were made up of frontiersmen from Tennessee and Kentucky, men who were expert at shooting the long rifles. Henry Hunter was one of these men. His home was in west Tennessee.

"While the battle was raging, the English general could be seen walking back and forth on the breastworks waving a sword and urging his men on. With his red coat, white ruffled shirt front, and white trousers, he made a splendid target. Now I quote old Henry: 'My officer came to me and said, "Hunter, can you see the General?" "Of course," I said. "Do you think you could bring him down from there?" "Well," I said, "I've killed many a deer on Half Pone (a small mountain in west Tennessee) as far away as he is." "Well, load your gun heavy and take careful aim, and see if you can get him." I did load heavy and got a good bead on his chest. When I fired he fell. Of course, others were shooting, and I never could be sure, but I heard afterwards that there was a wound right where I held.'

"It was the general's express wish that should he be killed in battle his body should be sent to England for burial, for he did not want to lie dead in rebel soil. In those days sailors were superstitious about carrying a corpse on board, so the officer in charge smuggled the body on board the ship. As no embalming was done in those days, they drew out about two-thirds of the contents from a barrel of rum, removed the corpse's head [since the body was too long to fit in the barrel], placed the body of the general inside, and placed the head beside the body. After this odoriferous work was finished, the barrel was hidden deep in the hold of the ship sailing for England.

"The passage was long and rough. The weather was stormy, the grog was not plentiful, and food was limited. The unhappy sailors did a lot of complaining.

"Finally an old salt went prowling around down in the ship and found the barrel in which the general was hidden. He reported to his mates as to how the officers were holding out on the men and hiding a whole barrel of rum for their own use. Since the men were just as smart as any officer, they soon had a gimlet, bored a hole in the barrel, and drew out enough each day for a little nip all around—on the sly, of course.

"The poor old general was almost dry when he was opened up for the funeral. When the sailors found out what had happened, they were sorry they had been so eager to doubt the motives of their officers.

"Anyway, it is said that all around the Gulf Coast that particular kind of rum is called 'Packenham.' "

From J. Russell Reaver, Florida Folktales *(Gainesville: University Presses of Florida, 1988), pp. 29–30; collected in the 1950s (the bracketed explanation is Reaver's).*

"A Mix-up in the Mail"

Grandmother had gone out to spend Christmas with her cousins who lived in the Far East. She had not seen them for several years and was very excited about the trip. They had always been very kind to her and each Christmas they used to send a present of a jar of special spices to go in the Christmas cake her daughter made.

About two weeks before Christmas, a small airmail parcel arrived from the Far East. It had been posted on 1 December and contained what appeared to be the special spices for the Christmas cake. There was no note with it nor, surprisingly, any Christmas card. Not wanting to delay any longer, the daughter got on with the baking and produced a magnificent cake for the Christmas festivities.

It was the day after Boxing Day that a letter arrived from the cousins in the Far East. Also dated 1 December, it expressed how sorry they were to have to break the news of grandmother's death—the excitement had been too much for her. They also wrote that, because of all the arrangements that had had to be made for the cremation, they would not have time to send over the special spices for the cake this year. However, they had airmailed grandmother's ashes home and they should arrive shortly.

From Paul Smith, The Book of Nasty Legends *(London: Routledge and Kegan Paul, 1983), p. 106. This widely told story is usually known as "The Accidental Cannibals" or "The Eaten Cremains."*

"The Face Is Familiar"

At the time of [Laurence] Sterne's death [1768] resurrectionists had been plying their ghastly trade in several London burial grounds, [which] made almost inevitable the most macabre of legends about the dead parson.

One day, the story runs, Dr. Charles Collignon, professor of anatomy at Cambridge, had invited some friends in to see the dissection of a corpse newly arrived from London. When the process was nearly finished, one of the visitors lifted the cloth that had concealed the head of the corpse. As he did so, he recoiled with horror. He had recognized the head of his friend, Laurence Sterne. The skull was said to have been kept (as indeed it would have deserved to be) as a great rarity; but among the collection at Cambridge it has never been identified. The complete disappearance of everything but the tradition should naturally cause the story to be treated with the greatest skepticism. Yet the tradition has been so persistent that it still finds credence in some quarters.

• • •

New Delhi teaching hospital. Jawahir Singh at his first dissecting class shouted out: "Stop! That's my mother," and fainted. It turned out that there was a mix-up at the local mortuary. Incident ended with apologies all around.

• • •

What is the percentage of a student's encountering a relative in the form of a cadaver in a gross anatomy laboratory? Such an event may occur in a science fiction novel or it may be the theme of a television production, but seldom does one have personal experience in such a coincidence. This unusual situation occurred earlier this year in the gross anatomy laboratory of a large southern university.

On the initial day of class the students were exposed to all nine of the cadavers. After the first day's dissection and before the beginning of the second laboratory session, the director of the course was informed of a potentially bizarre occurrence. A student informed the director that the distinct possibility existed that one of the cadavers (not the one she was dissecting) was a great aunt. At a meeting of the student and instructor before the second day of the laboratory it was ascertained that the cadaver was indeed her great aunt. The coincidence was further compounded when it was revealed that the cadaver had been shipped to the state anatomical board by the corresponding board of another state. Another interesting point was that the student and her great aunt had discussed the relative merits of body donation to medical science. Further trauma to the student was obviated by the immediate substitution of another cadaver by the state anatomical board.

The first story, one of several accounts of this alleged incident concerning the English novelist, is from Lodwick Hartley, This is Lorence: A Narrative of the Reverend Laurence Sterne *(Chapel Hill: The University of North Carolina Press, 1943), p. 271. The second brief, typical item, from the New Delhi hospital, is from a clipping from* World Medicine, *1973, sent to me by Dr. T. Healey of Barnsley, South Yorkshire, England. The third item was a letter to the editor published in the* Journal of the American Medical Association 247, no. 15 (April 16, 1982): p. 2096, signed by two faculty members of the University of Alabama School of Medicine in Birmingham.

"The Lost Wreck"

Miette Skeleton Mystery as Real as Mountain Mist

JASPER [Alberta, Canada]—The mystery of the Miette Hot Springs Road, along with the four human skeletons who made the tale so intriguing, can finally be laid to rest.

Like many a tantalizing story which gains credibility with repeated tellings, this rumor seems to have sprung from a fertile imagination fed by the clean mountain air.

A story doesn't have to be true to be told again and again.

According to one resident who preferred to remain nameless, a friend of a friend heard about a gruesome discovery made by a work crew widening the road to Miette Hot Springs over the summer.

"They were killing time over lunch by pushing boulders over the edge when they heard one of the rocks hitting metal.

"That got them interested. When they went down to look, they found this car with 1950s license plates and four skeletons inside."

As the story goes, for reasons never explained, authorities

wanted to keep the discovery a secret. Of course the hint of a cover-up simply added zest to the tale.

Don Dumpleton, Jasper's chief warden, chuckled when asked about the mystery before he explained there is no truth to the story.

"I've heard the story. The only thing is the place keeps changing," he said.

RCMP [Royal Canadian Mounted Police] Staff Sgt. Don Rumple vaguely recalled hearing the story but added police haven't encountered any lost cars or weathered skeletons while keeping watch on the tourists.

"I can guarantee you there was no such incident," added Corp. Kevin Fitzpatrick.

Ken Sawka, who operates the Miette Bungalows at the end of the road to the hot springs, said he heard the story during the late summer.

"I heard the rumor over coffee. Someone came up one day and said: 'What about those bodies they found up on your road?'

"Then I heard it was possible they found a car body and no skeletons on the Maligne Lake Road.

"It would be an interesting story—if it were true," he laughed.

And so another mystery story, like those rumors of corporations dealing with the devil or kidnappers cruising for victims in sinister black vans, evaporates into the mists swirling about the mountain peaks.

A story bylined by Paul Cashman from the Edmonton Journal, *December 15, 1985; partially quoted in* Too Good to Be True, *p. 235.*

"The Death Car"

A white fellow from around here, named Demings, committed suicide in his car back in 1938. He had a 1929 Model-A Ford, painted all over with birds and fish; it would catch your eye right away. He was going with a girl who didn't care much for him, Nellie Boyers, and it seems they had a fight when he took her on a date to the Iona State Fair. When he came back he pulled off the road into the brush, stuck a gas hose onto the tailpipe, turned the motor on, and sniffed the other end of the hose. He must have prepared for it, because he had the cracks under the seat and on the floorboards all chinked up with concrete, to keep the gas from escaping. He killed himself in August, and no one found him till October, in the hunting season. A guide kept going out to that spot where Demings had parked; he'd see the car and say, "That fellow's always hunting when I am." Finally he took a close-up look, and smelled the body.

A used-car dealer in Remus sold the car at a reduced price to Clifford Cross. Cliff did everything possible to get the smell out; he upholstered it, fumigated it, but nothing worked, and in the middle of winter he would have to drive around with the window wide open. I said one time, "If I'm going to freeze to death driving with you I'd rather be out on my feet," and I got out. Another time a little white dog crawled inside while Cliff was getting gas, and started to bark from the back seat after he drove off. Cliff thought it was the dead man's ghost, and he stopped that car and shot out like the Devil was after him. Finally he give up trying to get the smell out, and turned the car in for junk.

From Richard M. Dorson, Negro Folktales in Michigan *(Cambridge, Mass.: Harvard University Press, 1956), p. 99, collected from John Berry*

*of Mecosta, who was born in 1921. Dorson surmised that this highly
detailed early version was the original of the ubiquitous story of the new
car with the persistent smell of death offered for sale at a low price. In
1956 Dorson commented, "Every folklore class I have taught contained
students who knew and believed this story"; it is still widely told, most
often nowadays about a smelly Corvette. I disputed Dorson's claim about
its origins, while acknowledging Dorson's important role in urban legend studies, in* The Truth Never Stands in the Way of a Good Story.

"The Body on the Car"

A story recently appeared in Ann Landers (which must be a
gold mine of urban legends), and I hope it isn't true. A
woman wrote in to tell of a friend whose husband was always
drinking and driving. One night, he goes out with the boys
and comes home very late, after his wife is in bed, and parks
the car in the garage. The next morning, he leaves to go to
work, but his wife notices that he's forgotten his lunch box
(or briefcase); she runs out just in time to see him backing out
of the garage, but as soon as she screams at him to wait, she
keels over in a dead faint. The man gets out of the car to see
what's wrong: There's a little girl (dead) embedded in his car's
grillwork.

Please, Ann, tell us it's just a story!

• • •

Members of a group called SADD (Students Against Drunk
Drivers) made a presentation to our eighth graders to
warn them about drinking drivers. The high school student
who told this story had heard it from another SADD member.

A man went to an office party one Friday after work. He
was drinking heavily. Time passed quickly and he was going

to arrive home late, so he called his wife to let her know. Instead of waiting up, she went to bed.

The man got home way after midnight and was extremely drunk. He was so drunk he passed out on the couch as soon as he walked into the living room. His wife awoke early the next morning and walked past him when she went outside to get the morning paper.

The man was awakened by the hysterical screams of his wife. Embedded in his car's front grill was the twisted body of an eight-year-old girl.

I asked the storyteller whether he thought it was a bit strange for an eight-year-old girl to be outside by herself at that hour, and he invented details on the spot in an attempt to make the story plausible.

The first item is from one of about three dozen letters I received from all across the United States after Ann Landers printed a letter telling this story on September 24, 1986, signed "Still Horrified in Portland." Ann's comment at the time was "What a grisly story! Bone-chilling, to say the least." One reader who wrote me included a copy of her response to Ann Landers pointing out the earmarks of an urban legend in the letter: "no direct source, a creepy lead-up, and a wonderfully grisly punchline with a moral." But I never saw a further comment about this story in later Ann Landers columns. The second item was sent to me by a reader in California in 1989. Actual occurrences of similar accidents do not change the fact that the widely told, unverified, stylized versions are just scary ULs.

"Off with Their Heads!"

From Ireland:

A motorcyclist was riding behind a lorry which was loaded with sheets of corrugated iron. They were driving along the

Naas Dual-Carriageway and were just reaching the end where the road narrows, and the biker decided to overtake the lorry. As he pulled out and started to accelerate, a sheet of iron came loose and slid off the back of the lorry, decapitating the rider. Due to the fact that the throttle was being held open, the motorcycle continued on past the lorry. The driver looked down from his cab and, seeing the headless motorcyclist, he had a heart attack. His lorry careened of the road and ran over a woman pushing her baby in a pram, killing them both.

• • •

From Australia:

A man caught a taxi, and the driver put his luggage in the boot as the passenger got into the backseat. On the journey the passenger wound down the window and stuck his head out. When the taxi driver pulled up at the address that the passenger had given, he looked around to find a headless man sitting upright with his hand on the frame around the window. The driver told the police, and they backtracked along the road that he had driven along. They found the passenger's head in the fork of a tree beside the road.

• • •

From England (?):

I overheard this story about two months ago on the campus of the University of Florida here in Gainesville.

Somewhere in England a new roller coaster ride was being opened. They strapped in some test dummies, ran them through, and everything seemed OK. So, later, at the official opening, all the local dignitaries climbed in to be the first passengers on this new ride. They took off, and everything seemed OK, but when the cars pulled into the unloading ramp, everybody aboard had been decapitated!

It seems that the test dummies were more compressible

than humans; they sort of folded down into the seats, but the humans stayed sitting upright and got caught on a structural cable that was too low over the tracks at one point.

• • •

From Canada ("Off with Their Arms!"):

This story was told to me by a friend of about the same age as me, when I was about six. We were in the backseat of a car going downtown when my mother turned around and told me to keep my arm in the window as a truck may come along and hit it. My friend then went on to say that he heard of a boy who never listened to his mother and when they got home this little boy took off his jacket, and his arm just fell off. I remember thinking that I didn't want to have my arm fall off! To this day I never put my arm out the window.

I heard the story again when I lived in Nova Scotia from 1974 to 1976, only this time the boy didn't say anything to his parents after the truck hit his arm. And when he got home he went right to his room, took off his jacket, and his arm fell off.

The Irish version was collected in Dublin in 1987 by folklorist Eilís Ní Dhuibhne, who sent me several modern Irish legends after we met at an international folklore conference. The Australian version was sent to me in 1986 by Matt Sayer, who gave as his address the improbable name "Tea Tree Gully." Bob Johnson of Gainesville, Florida, sent me the supposed English version in 1986. The Canadian version was sent to me in 1989 by Bill Shropshire of Winnipeg, Manitoba.

"The Body in the Bed"

This was told to me by a friend who had heard it from a friend she was visiting in Arizona in 1992. The Arizona woman said this had happened to a friend of hers. This woman with a few friends had decided to visit Las Vegas for three days to do some gambling and generally imbibe some of the lively culture there. They checked in at the Mirage Hotel and Casino and went up to their room to drop their luggage. But they noticed a peculiar smell in the room, as if maybe the trash hadn't been taken out or the toilet had gone unflushed. Still, all seemed to be in order, so they left and did not return until late that evening.

The smell had gotten noticeably worse over the course of the day, so they called housekeeping to ferret out the offending odor. A housekeeper looked under the beds, in the closets, even sniffed out drains and vents, but could not pinpoint the smell's origin. Finally, they vacuumed the room with a generous amount of Carpet Fresh, turned the vent on high, and bade the Arizona women good night. The stench was masked for the moment, and, because they were all exhausted, they just went to bed. The woman who had told my friend's friend the story, as was her habit when in hotels, put her wallet underneath the mattress; then they all dabbed a bit of perfume on their upper lips and turned out the lights.

They all slept until late morning when the sun came streaming into the room, making it uncomfortably warm. The stench was still there to haunt them, now more potent than ever. Quite perturbed, one woman rang housekeeping once again to complain. Then she called the management office and complained some more. A small army of management and cleaning personnel arrived shortly, and again they looked high and low, but to no avail. All agreed, however, that the stench was overpowering, so the manager offered to put the women in another room. They packed up their things to move down the hall, but when the one woman reached beneath the mattress to retrieve her wallet, she seized upon something that felt suspiciously like a human hand.

The mattress was pulled off the bed, and there, lying in a hollowed-out spot in the box springs was a dead man. Evidently the man had been murdered in the room, and the murderer had hidden the body between the mattrress and box spring. He had cut out enough of the box springs and the underside of the mattress so the body wouldn't make a suspicious lump in the bed.

The Mirage Hotel management tried to calm the women by offering them three free nights in the hotel and about $1,500 of gambling credit in the casino.

Sent to me in March 1993 by Beverly J. Kelly of Covina, California. A news item circulated by the Associated Press in mid-July 2003, datelined Kansas City, told of a body found under a mattress in "the Capri Motel, just east of downtown" after "a guest had spent three nights [in the room], complaining repeatedly about a foul odor." A call to the Kansas City Police Department verified the incident, which seems to be a case of what we might call "a fulfilled urban legend."

"The Stuffed Baby"

My sister's co-worker has a sister in Texas who with her husband was planning a weekend trip across the Mexican border for a shopping spree. At the last minute their baby sitter canceled, so they had to bring along their two year old son with them. They had been across the border for about an hour when the baby got free and ran around the corner. The mother went chasing, but the boy had disappeared. The mother found a police officer who told her to go to the gate and wait. Not really understanding the instructions, she did as she was instructed. About 45 minutes later, a man approached the border carrying the boy. The mother ran to him, grateful that he had been found. When the man realized it was the boy's mother, he dropped the boy and ran himself. The police were waiting for him and got him. The boy, was dead, in less than 45 minutes he was missing, cut open, ALL of his insides removed and his body cavity stuffed with COCAINE. The man was going to carry him across the border as if he were asleep. A two year old boy, dead, discarded as if he were a piece of trash for somebody's cocaine. If this story can get out and change one person's mind about what drugs mean to them, We are helping. Please send this E-mail to as many people as you can, if you have a home PC send it out there too. Lets hope and pray it changes a lot of minds. The saddest thing about the whole situation is that those persons who suffer are innocent and people we love............God Bless you in this united effort to spread the word. You just might save a life!

An e-mail I received several times in 2000, reproduced here verbatim.

"The White Dress"

It was the night before the senior prom and one girl didn't have a dress to wear. She was poor and lived in the section of town where there were many immigrants from Haiti and other island countries in the Carribbean Sea. She had gone to the neighborhood funeral parlor that same day to pay her respects to an elderly neighbor who had died. While there, she had entered a room by mistake and had seen a young girl, about her age and size, lying in a casket. As she looked down at the casket, she noticed that the girl's dress was very pretty and brand-new. It had been probably bought just for the burial.

Then the funeral director came in and said it was time to close the casket. He sealed it with a big key, like a wrench, and said that the casket would remain closed from then until the burial the next morning. After the director left, the girl went down the hall to the room where her dead neighbor was laid out.

While she was in the viewing room paying her respects, she heard a lot of crying and wailing down the hall. Someone had collapsed with grief, and everyone, including the funeral director, ran down the hall to help the family. As the girl ran by the room with the sealed casket she had an idea.

She darted into the room, opened the sealed casket with the huge, curved wrench, and quickly slid the white dress off the body in the casket. She put the key back in the socket of the casket lid and sealed the lid again.

Stuffing the white dress into her school bag, she slipped out past the room where all the crying was coming from.

The next night, she put on the dead girl's white dress and went to the dance.

As she danced with several different boys she knew, her joints started to get stiff. As time went by, her muscles too began to stiffen, and she found herself walking and dancing awkwardly. She thought maybe there was something wrong with the dress.

She went into the girls' restroom and slipped into a stall. She took off the dress and searched it all over, but couldn't find anything wrong, so she put it back on.

As she danced some more, she became colder and stiffer, until finally she was as stiff as a board. An ambulance was called and she was rushed to the hospital, where the doctors pronounced her dead.

But she was alive! She could hear every word that was being said and see everything that was happening. She just couldn't move and couldn't speak.

Soon she was lying in the same funeral parlor where the

girl in the white dress had been laid out, with her family and friends coming by and weeping. She tried to move or cry out, but she couldn't.

The funeral director came and closed the lid on her casket.

The next day the casket was taken to the graveyard. She could hear the gravediggers working.

"Did you hear what happened at the funeral home this morning?" asked one.

"No, what?" asked the other, as they threw shovelfuls of dirt onto the casket.

The first gravedigger answered, "A young mortician's assistant heard a knocking sound in one of the caskets. He opened it and a young girl in a slip climbed out. She said she had been the victim of a voodoo ritual. Someone had given her a dress dusted with zombie powder, so she seemed dead when she wasn't."

"I wonder what happened to the dress?" said the other.

And then the girl in the casket couldn't hear anything else.

A professional storyteller's version of "Embalmed Alive" (see Chapter 1); concluding the story by describing the viewpoint of the victim is not characteristic of the traditional UL, although it's very effectively done here. From Richard and Judy Dockrey Young, Scary Story Reader *(Little Rock: August House, 1993), pp. 160–62, where it is noted that "there are many versions of this story, but they usually involve embalming fluid."*

ALONG CAME A SPIDER . . . OR A SNAKE, OR A RAT

Why do spiders and snakes seem so scary in horror legends? The Swedish folklorist Bengt af Klintberg, some of whose stories are quoted in this chapter, suggests that their rarity in the modern urban environment "has had the consequence that they have come to assume mythical proportions in our narrative traditions" ("Legends and Rumours about Spiders and Snakes," *Fabula: Journal of Folktale Studies* 26, nos. 3–4 [1985]: p. 287). Maybe so, but possibly it also has something to do with their *legs*—too many in the case of spiders, none at all in the case of snakes. Could it be the way spiders and snakes skitter or slither along that makes them seem so horrible? Whatever the reason, they share the scene with ants, maggots, roaches, rats, scorpions, and other such creepy creatures in horror ULs.

Klintberg, my Swedish counterpart, also sees these particular creatures as "symbols of the wildness and potential danger of the Third World," since so many of them in the stories are said to have arrived as imports from poorer countries (p. 286). He points out that their threat is often directed toward women and children, the assumed innocents in our modern world. Thus we find spiders, snakes, and their kin infesting hairdos, facial injuries, sinus cavities, tummies, house plants, fast-food restaurants, amusement parks, and, in one rumor of the late 1970s, even a popular bubble gum brand. (People could not agree, however, whether Bubble Yum was supposed to have contained spider *eggs* or spider *legs*.)

Helmut Fischer, the German folklorist whose version of "The Rat-Dog" I include, sees the invasion of the modern home by the stray rodent—mistaken for a small dog—as a case in which "the untamed has crossed the boundaries of civilization and become a threat." Once the creepy creature is recognized for what it is, it has to go:

> Without any further thought we give up the attempt to comprehend the Other on its own terms. We eliminate it by superior means and retreat once again behind the safe boundaries of civilization. The whole experience has brought us no insight into exotic foreign cultures, but rather has strengthened our prejudiced sense of our own superiority. (Page 203 of the translation cited with his text)

While most of us might welcome some "insight into exotic foreign cultures," I think we must draw the line at adopting rats.

Some of these stories have caused considerable concern among certain businesses. The "Snake in the Blanket" legend became so bothersome for K-Mart stores that the *Wall Street Journal* reported on October 7 and 20, 1981, that the company had started keeping track of inquiries about snakes in imported coats or blankets and assigned people to respond to the public's and journalists' requests for information. Newspapers have actually been quite conscientious in debunking such stories, ranging from C. Clairborne Ray's "Cactus and Spiders" column in the November 30, 1993, *New York Times*, which quoted from

scientific and folkloristic authorities, to many other local writers who produce articles like Thom Marshall's column in the
Houston Chronicle on July 20, 1990, which began on a light-
hearted note, "Fangs for the memories," and then debunked a
local snake story, bluntly labeling it "Completely untrue.
False. Balderdash."

The resilience of infestation legends through time is
remarkable. Consider that a version of "The Spider in the
Hairdo" circulated in the fourteenth century, describing the
devil in the form of a spider attaching himself to the elaborate
hairdo of a woman who was habitually late for Mass because
of the time it took to arrange her tresses. Nowadays, the
story—substituting cleanliness for godliness—is sometimes
attributed to a person wearing dreadlocks who has not
washed his or her hair for weeks. Similarly, the "Snake in the
Blanket" story has been updated from the simple coverlets of
yesteryear to the electric blankets of today (compare the
first story under the heading "Snakes in Dry Goods"). In
1840, when gummed postage stamps were introduced in
England, the rumor circulated that the glue on them would
give people cholera if they licked them. In November 2002 I
got an e-mail repeating a current warning about licking envelope flaps:

A co-worker told me that she never does that because of
something that happened to someone she knew. This person
supposedly cut her tongue while sealing envelopes, and several
weeks later had an infection in her tongue. She went to the doctor and they found that a bunch of maggots were living inside
her tongue. There had been insect eggs in the envelope glue.

(There's another e-mailed version of this story in Chapter
9, so brace yourself.)

New variations on these themes continue to be hatched. The *New York Times* reported on July 31, 2001, that the Centers for Disease Control and Prevention maintains a space on their Web site just to debunk the rampant rumors of, as the newspaper put it, "the dreaded arachinius gluteus, a spider said to lurk beneath toilet seats waiting to bite those who sit." The CDC felt it had to get involved when word of mouth and e-mails "cited the health centers as a source of information."

That truth in these matters is sometimes stranger than fiction is proved by a scientific report that's as horrible as the worst of the urban legends about infestations in the body. Paul D. Hurd, Jr., an entomologist working at the Arctic Research Laboratory, in Point Barrow, Alaska, reported a harrowing personal experience in dry academic prose under the headline " 'Myiasis' Resulting from the Use of the Aspirator Method in the Collection of Insects" (*Science,* June 4, 1954). "Myiasis"—are you ready for this?—refers to "infestations with fly maggots," and Mr. Hurd suffered from an infestation in his sinuses when a faulty piece of collecting equipment allowed eggs and larvae of the specimens he was collecting to enter his nasal passages. He even counted the inhabitants once he had sniffed them out, so to speak; skipping the scientific names here, he tabulated three adult rove beetles, thirteen fungus gnat larvae, three parasitic wasp eggs, and about fifty springtails. Now *that's* scary!

"The Spider in the Hairdo"

When I was in high school (1962–66) bouffant, or "beehive," hairdos were the rage among teenage girls. These arrangements featured the hair piled high and held in place with a copious covering of tough hairspray. Getting the hair wet deflated the hairdo.

When I heard this story I was living in East Palo Alto, California. The story went that a woman at Stanford University had an elaborate beehive hairdo, and to keep her hair in place she sprayed it daily. She did not wash her hair for a month, and when she tried to wash it at last, she died quickly. In the pile of hair on her head was the nest of a black widow spider; the spider bit her when she wet her hair.

• • •

Another ending:

. . . one day at school, while she was seated in class, she suddenly began to convulse, screaming and tearing at her hair as if stricken with some kind of insanity. Eventually she collapsed unconscious, and her classmates rushed to her aid.

They saw a trickle of blood seeping out from under her hair, and they promptly summoned the school nurse. By the time the nurse arrived, the girl was dead.

The coroner, in his postmortem, broke open the beehive hairdo and discovered over two dozen baby redback spiders there. A female redback had got into her hairdo, then laid eggs; the eggs hatched, and the young spiders started eating the flesh of the girl's scalp, eventually boring right into her brain.

The story came from Mary K. Wicksten of Bryan, Texas, who sent it to me in 1984. The second ending, typical of most versions, came from Bob Rasmus of Australia in 1986.

"The Spider Bite"

A girl I know from Glasgow went on holiday with friends to the coast of North Africa—she had a terrific time. The only problem they had during the visit was on the last day when they had an invasion of small insects—particularly spiders. These appeared to have been blown out to the coast from the desert and all you could do was to keep brushing them away.

In spite of this they managed to get a few hours sun-bathing in, during which my friend was bitten on her face by the spiders a couple of times. Thinking no more about it, she simply applied an antiseptic cream to the bites and forgot about them.

By the time she had returned to Glasgow the bites were looking rather inflamed and beginning to look like boils. In spite of further treatment, they refused to subside so she eventually thought it best to arrange to visit the doctor the following day.

Going to the bathroom the next morning she saw in the

mirror that the bites looked even worse. She had just begun to carefully wash her face when she felt a sharp pricking sensation. Looking in the mirror again she was horrified and began to scream hysterically. The boils had burst and crawling all over her face and in her hair were hundreds of tiny baby spiders.

From Paul Smith, The Book of Nastier Legends *(London: Routledge and Kegan Paul, 1986), pp. 40–41, titled there "A Present from the Seaside."*

"Quit Bugging Me!"

This woman felt something moving around in her ear—her *right* ear—and there was this sort of buzzing sound that was driving her crazy. She guessed that maybe an earwig had crept in when she was lying on the grass in her backyard sunbathing, but eventually the sound stopped, so she figured it must have got out again. But then her head started aching, and she started feeling sick and dizzy; soon a new intense pain started to come from around her *left* ear, so she went to see a doctor about it. The doctor listened to her description of the new ear problems and decided that it probably *was* an earwig; in fact, he pulled one out of the left ear with a thin little tweezer. It was a female earwig with some eggs and babies following it out, so he concluded that this little bug must have gone in on the right, bored on through her brain—laying eggs all the way—and then come out the other side of her head. The woman went crazy from the horror of that idea, besides which her brain had been permanently damaged.

• • •

There was this little kid, maybe about two or three years old, that kept crying and saying that something was hurting her in her head—around her forehead, between her eyes. She kept scratching at her forehead and crying and complaining, and finally—driven nuts by the pain—she jabbed a fork into her forehead one day when she was eating. And a stream of ants came running out that had been living in her sinuses.

• • •

The way I heard it was that the little kid had a broken arm or leg and kept complaining that there was a terrible itching under the cast, so she kept trying to scratch with a knitting needle or a stick or something. But the doctor said she would just have to endure it until the cast had been on long enough—something like six weeks. He said it was OK to scratch under the cast, though. So, when they finally took the cast off they found that the little girl's leg (or arm) was infested with maggots, or maybe termites, and the limb had to be amputated.

• • •

After going on dozens of diets without losing any weight, a young woman finally decided to try diet pills. They made her lose so much weight all at once that she was really happy about it. Then one night, while she was lying in bed, she felt something move in her head, and a tapeworm crawled right out of her nose!

Common rumors and legends about insect infestations of the body, all with, perhaps, just a grain of truth, or at least possibility.

"Spiders in Cacti"

Sweden, 1975; told by a man in Spånga, a suburb of Stockholm:

A man and a woman had been abroad and they had brought back a little cactus in a pot to Sweden. One night some months later the woman woke up when something fell down to the floor. It was the pot with the cactus. In its place she now saw a spider. She became terrified and awoke her husband, and they both ran out of their bedroom. Then they called the police and asked them to send a patrol car to their apartment. But no car was available, and instead they were advised to try to catch the spider in a coffee can or something like that, and put something over the opening.

The couple opened a can of coffee and poured out the coffee in order to get an empty can. Then they returned to their bedroom on shivering legs and succeeded in capturing the spider in the can. They put a piece of paper over the opening, and the man called the police again, asking them what to do with the can. While he was still talking on the telephone, the woman started to scream. The spider was eating its way through the paper.

Later the police came and fetched the can, which was taken to some institution for analysis. It appeared to be a spider with a capacity of spitting venom up to three metres, a venom that is fatal when just touching human skin. It could eat through any material except steel. It had probably been lying immobile in the cactus until it was fully grown and then found its way out.

• • •

Sweden, 1984; published in the Gothenburg newspaper *Göteborgs-Posten*:

Watch out when you buy a yucca palm. You might get a poisonous spider in the bargain. This is what a lady in Gothenburg experienced. One day the stem of her palm cracked and out tumbled a big hairy black spider, poisonous on top of that. Since spiders were not among her favorite pets, she immediately called the police. The woman was sitting in her living-room when she heard a sudden bang. A closer investigation showed that her big yucca palm had burst in two pieces. Imagine her fright when she then saw the spider.

The woman had the presence of mind to put the palm with the spider on her balcony while she waited for the police to come. A policeman could catch the little monster quickly and easily with the help of a net.

When the woman called the police some days later she was informed that the spider, according to their investigations, was poisonous. What happened to the spider is not on record.

. . . Because of this single case one cannot draw the conclusion that all yucca palms hide poisonous spiders, experts in this field say.

• • •

Sweden, 1984; in a letter from a postman in the town of Skellefteå:

There was a woman in Skellefteå who had bought a yucca palm. When looking at it in the kitchen she had a funny feeling that it was moving in one direction. She thought that it might depend on her not having given it enough water, so she watered it, but it still moved.

She watered it once again. Then the palm moved in another direction. She now called the florist, "The Bouquet," in Skellefteå, where she had bought the plant. At "The Bouquet" they answered that she should immediately close the doors to the kitchen, because at once they knew that there was a poisonous spider in the pot. And not just a little poisonous, extremely poisonous.

—We will come immediately, said the representative of the florist. Part of the story is that a person in an outfit resembling that of an astronaut came to render the spider harmless.

• • •

Minnesota, 1991; told by a nineteen-year-old female student at the University of Minnesota, Morris:

You know what happened to this girl my mom works with? She had bought one of those big cactuses from Bachman's [a floral store chain in the Twin Cities area], you know. A really big one, about as tall as me [about five feet seven inches], with the pot, and about this big around [hands indicate about a twelve-inch-diameter circle].

Well, she had it delivered and she set it out in front of her other plants, in this big picture window. She had it for a few days, and one night after work she was reading a book in her living room, where the picture window was, and she looked up and noticed that her cactus was, like, undulating. [Teller waves fingers up and down.] Mostly on the bottom half, the thing was *moving*.

So she got up and called her mom and her mom said "get out of the house *now*, and call the police. I'll call the bomb squad and be right over." And the girl called the police from her front yard; she had a cordless phone, I guess, and they came and the bomb squad and the girl's mother came, and the bomb squad put the cactus back into this big tall box that it had been delivered in, and just as they got it shut the cactus exploded with hundreds of baby tarantulas. It was full of tarantula eggs that whole time! [Teller pauses for audience reaction.]

I think Bachman's gave her a full refund.

• • •

Originally, Dublin, Ireland, 1998; an e-mail forwarded at least three times en route to me. Verbatim text, minus names, addresses and forwarding codes:

Subject: Fwd: Plantlife
    Another urban legend making the rounds . . .
    No more house plants for me . . .
    This actually happened to a buddy of the guy who sits next to me here in work . . .

Here's one I heard last night...and IT IS TRUE!
A friend of mine bought a tropical plant in Arnotts about 2 weeks ago-from South America I think, big green leaves, etc. She brought it home and placed it in her bedroom on the windowsill.

After 2 days, the plant withered and died, so my friend decided to bring It back to Arnotts and look for her money back.

Two days later, a van pulled up outside her house, and 6 guys dressed in "spacesuits" knocked on her door, said they were from Govt. agency, and started to fumigate her entire house.........just picture the scene from E.T right!?

It turns out that Arnotts had found the decomposed body of a male Black Widow spider in the leaves of the tropical plant my friend returned. And for those of you who don't know about black widows, seemingly the female kills the mail just after they have...........done it.

It was feared tht the male might have been killed recently, and that the female might be in my friends house.

She was-they found her in the duvet cover in the bedroom where the plant had been left for 2 days-and she had already laid her eggs!

Happy Easter!

-John

The Swedish versions are from an article by Bengt af Klintberg, "Legends and Rumours about Spiders and Snakes," Fabula: Journal of Folktale Studies 26, nos. 3–4 (1985): pp. 282–84. The Minnesota version was sent to me by the collector Jennifer Johnson, in 1997; at that time she was a graduate student taking a folklore course at Moorhead State University and reviewing texts she had collected as an undergraduate at the University of Minnesota, Morris. The e-mailed version was forwarded by senders with generic electronic addresses, but the original's source, "John," listed at the end a business address in Dublin, Ireland.

"Snakes Alive!"

It's my brother's wife who told me this, and it happened outside Borås [a town in western Sweden]. A woman friend of hers had bought a bunch of bananas. She gave her little kid a banana and said:

"Now you sit here and eat this banana."

Then she went into the kitchen. There she could hear him shouting:

"Mum, something is moving inside the banana!"

"Yeah, sure," said the mother, "the banana is alive. Sure!"

She thought that this was just something he imagined. But then she found him dead. He had been bitten to death by a little snake, just 4–5 centimetres long, a miniature cobra.

Since I heard this, I always take a good look before eating bananas to make sure there is no snake in them.

• • •

About a week ago, a mother took her eager 3 year old son to a fast food chain's restaurant for lunch. After they ate their lunch the mother said that the son could go and play on the playground for awhile since he ate all his lunch. She watched as the boy played in the tunnels, slide and in the **ball-pit.** The boy played for about 10 minutes when he started to wimper slightly. The mother asks the boy what had happened and he merely replied, "Hurt mommy." The mother assumed that the little boy had banged his elbow or somethng while playing. They left to return home. A half an hour later they were home, the mother noticed some big red welts on the little boy's arms and legs. Not being able to figure out what they were, the mother started to look at them close. Could be red ant bites . . . she did not know. An hour later the little boy died.

She came to find out, when returning to the fast food restaurant to see if there were red ants in the play area, in case the little boy had an allergic reaction, that there was a family of baby rattlesnakes living underneath the balls in the ball-pit area. She has since found out that this **can** happen! The snakes will crawl into the ball-pit because it is dark and warm in there. She knows for a fact that another death has occurred because of this in South Carolina.

Please use caution when letting any children play in an outside play area of a fast food restaurant, this could happen anywhere.

The restaurant in question is now building their play area **inside** the buildings for a safer environment.

• • •

My grandmother told me this:

You know the lady who lives over on Ave. N? Well she and her husband were at the Fiesta Mart [a supermarket chain] and she was going through the bananas when she felt something bite her finger. A few minutes later she felt light-headed and went to the car to lie down. When her husband arrived minutes later he found her dead. Upon further investigation it was found that the bananas she was looking through last were from Honduras and there was this little poisonous snake hiding amongst them.

The first story is from Bengt af Klintberg, "Legends and Rumours about Spiders and Snakes," Fabula: Journal of Folktale Studies 26, nos. 3–4 (1985): p. 276. It was included in a 1976 letter from a fifteen-year-old girl from Jakobsberg, west of Stockholm. The second story is a verbatim transcript of an undated and unidentified clipping from a local free newspaper sent to me in 1998 by Elisabeth Evans of Harrisburg, Pennsylvania. The third story came in a 1990 letter from Chris Pinon of Houston, Texas.

"Snakes in Dry Goods"

While I was teaching in Orchard park I was told this story by one of the teachers there. A woman and her husband had gone shopping to one of the discount houses in this area where they were looking for an electric blanket. The woman slid her hand into the blanket to feel it. As she did this, she felt something prick her finger. She thought that it was some sort of wire sticking out from the blanket. After looking around a while, they went home. In the middle of the night, the woman woke up with a strange feeling in her arm. When she looked at it she found that it was swollen. Her husband immediately took her to the hospital. Because of some reason unknown to them, the woman's arm had to be amputated. The doctor asked the husband what they had done that day. The husband retold eveything including the part about the blanket. They went back to the store and had it opened up so that they could check the boxes which held the blankets. Upon opening one of the boxes and examining the blankets, they found a mother cobra and three baby cobras. This was the strange occurrence that could have taken a woman's life.

•　•　•

Did you hear what happened last Friday at K-Mart? A woman was trying on these fake fur coats that they were unpacking from Taiwan. She thought she scratched her neck on a tag and immediately felt so sick she got her husband to walk with her out to the parking lot. When she fell unconscious, they rushed her to the emergency room at Shannon Hospital. Finally, doctors determined she had been bitten by a cobra. Back in the boxes of coats at K-Mart they found a whole bunch of baby cobras that had hatched out in the linings of the garments during shipments. The woman is in critical condition and isn't expected to live. A friend of my sister's neighbor was in the store just after it, and I hear the store is trying to keep it quiet and is paying off the family.

•　•　•

A mother went to Kmart to purchase a winter coat for her son. The young boy had been fussing on the way to the store and most of the day as well. Inside the store the boy kept up his ill-tempered behavior. They went straight to the children's coat section and located a rather inexpensive coat for him, but the little boy did not want to try the coat on. At this point, the mother lost her patience and forced the child into the coat. He began crying louder and causing a commotion, and she was upset at his behavior and finally removed the coat.

So she purchased the coat and got the boy home as soon as possible. Some time later the boy was still very cranky, but subdued, and he had developed a rash. As the rash increased, the boy became even quieter, and the mother, fearing that he had caught some kind of virus, rushed her son to the hospital. There the doctors diagnosed the rash as caused by the bite of a snake, or possibly several snakes.

The mother was asked to think back over the day and recall anything that might have been peculiar. Then she remembered the incident at Kmart, and she told them about the events in the store. They told her to bring in the coat, and she remembered leaving it in the back of the car when she took the boy into the hospital. She brought in the coat, still in its original bag. They opened the bag and saw that the coat was moving! They tore open the coat and found a nest of snakes inside. The coat had been made in Korea.

The first story is from Patrick B. Mullen, "Department Store Snakes," Indiana Folklore *3, no. 2 (1970): pp. 218–19, as told by a student at the State University College, Buffalo, New York, in 1969. The second is from Ann Carpenter, "Cobras at K-Mart: Legends of Hidden Danger,"* Publications of the Texas Folklore Society *40 (1976): pp. 38–39, as told by a student at Angelo State College, in Texas, in 1974. The third story was collected by a student of mine at the University of Utah, in Salt Lake City, in 1985.*

"The Creeping Comforter"

My brother told me last year about a woman who buys an eiderdown [a down-filled comforter] for a suspiciously low price. She is very pleased with it and puts it on her bed. When she enters the bedroom again, it has slipped to the floor, so she replaces it. The first time she sleeps under the new eiderdown she wakes up in the middle of the night because the thing has slipped from the bed once more. Finally, she opens the cover to have a look at the quilting, and she discovers that it is full of maggots. Flies have laid eggs in the blood that was sticking to the chicken feathers, which, rather than real eiderdown, were used for the filling.

Quoted as "The Contaminated Comforter" in my Encyclopedia of Urban Legends, *this legend came from Peter Burger of Leiden, Holland, who sent it to me in 1990; I like the story so much I could not resist repeating it here. Burger published another version with a note, "Het Wandelende Dekbed," in his 1992 book* De Wraak van De Kangoeroe: Sagen uit het moderne Leven *(The Kangaroo's Revenge: Legends of Modern Life), speculating that it may be a "uniek Nederlandse moderne sagen" (a unique Dutch urban legend); so far, I have not found any "maggoty quilt" stories elsewhere.*

"The Snake in the Strawberry Patch"

On Monday of this week, a friend of mine who operates a pick-your-own strawberry farm called. She was quite disturbed. Someone had started a rumor about an incident at her farm in which a young family with a baby was out picking strawberries. The baby, it seems, was left in a toddler seat while the mother and father were some distance away in the strawberry field. When they returned, they found that the baby had been killed by a snake that had either crawled down its throat or strangled it. Or so the story goes.

• • •

Lorrie Ostrowski told a tale "the girl at work swore is true."

A woman, with her 2-week-old infant beside her, was driving a pickup truck in the Tappahonnock area. The woman decided to stop on the side of the road to pick strawberries and briefly left her son in the truck with a bottle of milk.

Returning to the truck a few minutes later, the woman noticed something black dangling from her newborn's mouth. The black object was the tail of a snake that had slithered down the baby's throat after the milk and killed the boy.

Now doesn't that story make you drop your fork?

• • •

MOSCOW (UPI)—Eleven-year-old Matanet woke up from a catnap in a tomato patch gripping her throat and choking, and doctors later removed a 2-foot-long snake the girl had swallowed in her sleep, the Communist Party newspaper *Pravda* said Wednesday.

Pravda said the incident took place in the village of Sabirabad in the Soviet Caucasian republic of Azerbaijan.

The girl, known only by her first name, Matanet, said she grew tired picking tomatoes one hot day and fell asleep.

The first two stories are from American journalists: the first came in a June 10, 1987, letter from William A. Dennis, managing editor of the Henderson *(North Carolina)* Daily Dispatch, *and the second is from Eileen Barrett's August 24, 1987, article in the* Richmond *(Virginia)* News Leader. *Both writers debunked the local versions. The third story was widely printed as a news item on August 20, 1987; when reported again in* Omni *in May 1990, it was described as something that had appeared "recently" in* Pravda, *with the details added that the girl was given "3.5 pints of a salt solution to drink" in order to drive from her stomach a "25.6 inch Caucasian rat snake."*

"Der Rattenhund" ("The Rat-Dog")

In April 1986 my sister (medical student in Würzburg, age 22) told me (history student, Bonn, age 25) at the family home in Cologne the story of the "Giant Rat of Thailand," as she had heard it from a female fellow student in March, 1986. That student had heard the story from a married couple that are friends of hers in Duisburg (the fellow student's hometown) in October, 1985. The married couple claimed to have heard the story directly from the people involved in it.

The married couple went to Thailand on vacation in the summer of 1985. During a pleasant walk around the city a small dog ran up to them. It wouldn't leave them, and they fed it from the leftovers of their lunch. Because it was so friendly, they decided to smuggle it into their hotel room. They fed it regularly and began to win its trust.

As the end of the trip approached, they decided to take the cute animal back to Germany, in their hand-carried luggage and without a vaccination. Since the animal never barked, and was so well-behaved, they didn't foresee any complications. And so they landed on Sunday in Germany without anybody noticing the animal.

But then they thought of a new problem, because their cat was waiting for them at home. But the cat and dog liked each other from the first moment and even ate out of the same bowl. So this worry was taken care of as well. So both of them went to work on Monday happy and contented and looking forward to a pleasant evening with both pets.

But when they opened the door of their apartment in the evening there lay before them the skeleton of their cat, picked clean. They decided to take the dog immediately to the veterinarian, who examined it thoroughly and determined that it was healthy. But he asked the couple where they had bought the animal. Since both of them were aware of the possible punishment for illegally bringing animals into the country, they answered that they had bought the dog in a business that trades with the zoo. But the doctor wouldn't give up, and even threatened to call the police. After a while the couple confessed that they had brought the animal from Thailand. The doctor nodded with satisfaction, and explained that they had brought not a dog, but a giant Thailand rat. The couple were disturbed and shocked, as they remembered with horror playing affectionately with the little dog. Then the doctor put the animal immediately to sleep.

Collected by German folklorist Helmut Fischer and published in a 1986 article, "Der Rattenhund: Das Beispiel einer neuen Sage." The English translation of the article, "The Rat-Dog: An Example of a 'New' Legend," appeared in Contemporary Legend: A Reader, *ed. Gillian Bennett and Paul Smith (New York: Garland, 1996), pp. 187–207, with this version appearing on pp. 193–94.*

POOR BABY!

Babies and young children are so small, so helpless, so innocent—just so darned *cute*—that any story suggesting danger to them is alarming to hear. The plots seem especially horrible if they sound like true accounts of something that could have been avoided. Welcome to the awful world of scary ULs about kiddies!

We have already seen examples of the "Poor Baby" theme in legends such as "The Babysitter and the Man Upstairs" (see the introduction and Chapter 2) and "The Stuffed Baby" (see Chapter 3). "The Snake in the Strawberry Patch," in Chapter 4, contains the theme in another form, and there's more— and worse—to come in this chapter.

Nobody would deny that bad things sometimes really do happen to babies; unfortunately, that's the way it is. But the much-repeated scary ULs are fantasy scenarios—stereotyped accounts of frightening and gruesome incidents that never occurred in exactly that way anywhere, no matter how many details are included or how specifically the attacks are localized in the tellings. Again and again, investigating authorities, whether police, journalists, or folklorists, have shown that most of the rumors and legends about ghastly dangers to children are just that—rumors and legends. There were no harried babysitters gassing the kids to put them to sleep; no hippies roasting babies in the oven; no disguising of toddlers in shopping malls by would-be abductors; no phantom clowns lurking in black vans around schools or playgrounds; and hardly any Halloween sadists sabotaging candy or fruit with needles or razor blades.

Aren't there enough real-life dangers to small children to concern us without adding the dangers related in such legends? Apparently not, because these legends have been rampant for generations. Centuries ago in Europe it was the Gypsies who were said to be stealing babies; at Christmastime in 1999 in northern Indiana and southwestern Michigan it was—guess who?—the Gypsies again, this time rumored to be stealing babies from Meijer stores.

Part of the reason for their popularity is that such legends serve as perfectly reasonable warnings against poor caregiving. We learn from them to keep an eye on the kids, check out their babysitters, safeguard their everyday environment, and teach them to resist potential attackers. Parents may become a little better at parenting after hearing repeated horror tales about inept caregivers or lurking criminals in public places. So what if the stories aren't literally true? They *could* happen, and they incorporate elements of truth, like the names of specific shopping centers or department stores. An account of mall-abduction stories from the South Bend, Indiana, area mentioned that, according to hearsay, one endangered child "had a blonde ponytail and was wearing pink corduroys" when she went into the mall with her mom but when rescued at the last minute "had short blonde hair and was wearing jeans." Who makes up this stuff?

Another factor in the popularity of "Poor Baby" legends is their psychological credibility. Characters in these particular legends may exhibit sibling rivalry, or they may demonstrate the normal ambivalent feelings of parents toward those little ones who depend on us for their health and safety but who are sometimes a big pain in the neck. The scariness of being lost or left home alone is real enough, even if the story about it isn't, and we all know that bad luck just naturally seems to come in threes (as in the "Inept Mothers" stories). Another common folkloristic motif in these legends is the notion of a conspiracy to cover up the danger; supposedly, that's why you never read about these crimes in the newspaper or see them reported on TV. Actually, rather than suppressing such stories, media often debunk local rumors and legends, usually to little avail. News articles and columns mocked the Norwegian "stuck baby" tale quoted in this chapter, for example, with the headline "Bjorn Yesterday"; another debunking was head-lined "Up a Creek without a Rattle."

Some local outbreaks of these legends can be very intense. When stories of an attempted abduction in Paramus, New Jersey, erupted in October of 1983, a Hackensack newspaper, *The Record*, reported that police had received more than two hundred telephone calls from worried citizens ("Paramus Buzzes with Rumors of Child Abductions," October 26, 1983). The chief of police was reported to have said, "I've personally gotten about 75 calls on these [rumors], plus the switchboard has received over 100, the detective bureau 20, and the juve-nile bureau 20." I could cite cases like this many times over for dozens of scare stories spread over many years and liter-ally from coast to coast; even speedier is the rapid Internet cir-culation of child-focused urban legends in recent years.

The last two legends in this chapter concern older children and are less well known. "The Hammered Child" is a story with a unique theme that came from my own community; the second is a firsthand report of a desperate suicide using pencils as weapons during a crucial exam, as told by a teenager from England in 1991. I know of at least one American counterpart to his "pencils as weapons" story from a letter that came to me from Philadelphia earlier the same year. There, I was told about a plucky schoolgirl who defended herself against a man who attacked her on the street by jabbing him in the eye with her eyeliner pencil, which she just happened to be holding in her hand as she walked home from school. Perhaps we should consider registering pencils or makeup as deadly weapons in addition to guns.

Speaking not just as a folklorist, but also as a parent and grandparent, I just cannot be too dismissive of the "Poor Baby" legends. Logically, I know they are fictional, but emotionally, they give me the willies.

"Harried Babysitters"

The basic plot is that a lady on a bus hears two young girls chatting in the seat behind her. They are talking about their problems handling kids when baby-sitting. One of the girls tells the other a method she uses of quieting any little kid who cries too much; she lays him down with head in oven, and opens the gas vent for a while. When he is drowsy, she puts him in the crib and never has a bit of trouble. If he gets too lively again, back into the oven he goes.

The lady on the bus is outraged. For one reason or another she can't find out who the girls are. This leaves the matter up in the air for full shock value.

• • •

In New York City you have to be awfully careful about getting babysitters. You just don't know what might happen. My sister's girlfriend was sitting in the subway one day when she heard two women discussing the kids they sat with and how they handled them. She heard one of them say, "I take them into the kitchen and give them just a l-l-ittle bit of gas."

. . .

When our children were young, twenty to twenty-five years ago, a friend was riding on a bus. She was sitting in front of two teenage girls who were discussing the problems of babysitting. When the subject turned to crying babies and how to stop their crying, one girl was overheard to say to the other, "That's no problem. I just turn on the gas in the oven, put the baby's head in until it falls asleep and then take it out." This story was accepted as gospel by young parents of the time.

. . .

Some parents expressed [their] concern by recounting the unfortunate experiences of friends or acquaintances with truly unreliable childcare workers. One woman cited an extreme example of a baby-sitter's negligence:

I have a friend who had a baby, and one day she forgot something at home. So she went home, and her childcare person had her baby's head in the oven. And she said, "What are you doing to my baby?" and the childcare person said, "Well, I always do this. He seems to sleep better." And this is someone who lived in her house for six months, and who knows what the hell she did?

The first version is from Jerome Beatty, "Funny Stories," Esquire, November 1970, p. 48. The second was sent to me many years ago by folklorist Ernest Baughman, who had collected it from a student in 1953. The third came in a letter from Charles Brown of Vero Beach, Florida, in 1980. The last version is quoted from Rosanna Hertz, More Equal Than Others: Women and Men in Dual-Career Marriages *(Berkeley: University of California Press, 1986), p. 178.*

"The Baby-Roast"

First student:

(I heard this from a friend who knew the person, and it is supposedly true.)

This couple had a brand-new baby, didn't want to go any place, but a friend talks them into getting a babysitter. So they get one, and they go to a party. Of course, the wife, being nervous their first time being away from the baby calls home and says "How's it doing?" and the girl sounded strange and said, "Your roast is done." She didn't remember anything about a roast, so they go home. . . .

Second student:

(My mother heard this same story at a Relief Society meeting from one of the sisters. It was supposed to have been in the newspaper.)

. . . when they arrived home, they could smell this awful sickening sweet smell. The mother rushed into the kitchen, and there she found the table set for two with her best china and crystal. The lights were out and there were lit candles on the table. In the oven was their baby! The girl had roasted the baby! She said, "Look, I fixed a special dinner for you."

First student again:

The girl had been on drugs and had freaked out and had cooked the baby in the oven.

If that's true, I'm sick! But, as I said, it was told from a reliable source.

A combination of two versions collected at Brigham Young University, Provo, Utah, in 1977, by students of Professor William A. Wilson. At that time, many were still calling the story "The Hippy Babysitter." The terms "Relief Society" and "sisters" refer to practices of the Church of Jesus Christ of Latter-day Saints, but this legend is known widely among Mormons and "Gentiles" (the Mormon term for non-Mormons) alike.

"Baby's Stuck at Home Alone"

Translated from Norwegian:

The story goes that a couple from Bergen have planned a vacation in the south of Europe, and they have arranged for someone to care for their little girl at home. The babysitter— or in some versions, the baby's grandmother—does not show up by the time the couple have to leave for the airport. But they take off anyway, leaving the baby securely fastened in its highchair. It turns out that the babysitter had suddenly become ill and was lying unconscious, while the baby sat alone in the house and eventually died.

•   •   •

An e-mail from Canada:

I heard this in Dartmouth, Nova Scotia, in about 1964–65 from my boyfriend's brother who claimed it happened to the cousins of one of his in-laws.

This young couple had a ten-month-old baby. They couple wanted to get away from Dartmouth for some winter sun in Florida. They knew the baby-sitter would be late, and when the taxi came to take them to the airport, they tied the sleeping baby in his highchair and left the front door unlocked. The baby- sitter went to the back door, found the door locked, and thought the parents had made other arrangements. When the parents came back ten days later, the highchair was knocked to the floor, the baby was dead, and his left fist had been gnawed off!

• • •

Avery young married couple heading for a vacation to Disney World have arranged for a teenage sitter to care for their baby in their apartment while they're gone. The sitter is late, and they're unwilling to miss their flight. So they tie the baby to its high chair in the belief that the sitter will show up soon. They prop open the door and leave.

A dog slips through the door and knocks the prop loose, so the door shuts the dog and the baby inside. The sitter finally appears, but as the door is locked, and no one answers her knock, she assumes they've taken the baby along, and she goes home.

The rest of the gruesome story involves the dog eating the baby . . . and so on.

The Norwegian story was published in the newspaper Bergens Tidende *on September 22, 1972, and quoted in an article by folklorist Reimund Kvideland, "Det stod i avisa!" (It was in the newspaper!) sent out as a Christmas greeting in 1973 (translation is mine). The e-mail from Canada came from Barbara Robinson of Nanaimo, British Columbia, in October 2002. The third story is from a January 1990 letter from Marlene Palmer of Elkhart, Indiana.*

"Inept Mothers"

My friend's sister told me this on March 25, 1986. She heard it somewhere back east and says it's true.

A mother with 3 small children was giving her 6 month

old baby a bath in the tub when her 2 year old cut himself very badly. She couldn't leave her baby in the water, so she told her 6 year old to run across the street to the neighbors and get help. It took so long that she left the baby to help the 2 year old, who was unconscious by now. She heard sirens, thinking help was there, but they were there because her 6 year old had been hit by a car. In the meantime, the baby in the tub drowned and the 2 year old bled to death. So she lost all 3 of her children in 20 minutes, thru no fault of her own.

• • •

I just heard a story relayed by an acquaintance whose mother had heard it from a friend of a friend.

A lady had a daughter of about five years old and she then gave birth to a little boy. One day the girl noticed that her brother was different anatomically to her and asked the mother why. The mother told her that God had forgotten to cut it off and therefore they had a little boy.

A few days later the mother was on the phone when the little girl came to her with something in her hand saying "See Mommy! See!" To the mother's horror it was the baby's penis. She rushed the baby into the car, and in her panic, forgot the little girl and backed over her with the car and killed her. This delayed getting the baby to the hospital and he died on the way.

• • •

Mother caught two-year-old Reggie playing with himself in the bathroom. She said:

"No, Reggie, I've told you before and I'm telling you again. If you don't stop that I'm going to cut if off with a knife."

Mother then began partially filling the tub to bathe six-month-old Clarice.

Hattie, who was four years of age, desperately wanted to impress Mother and make her think better of her and less of the new baby. When she overheard Mother again telling Reggie what she'd do, she followed Reggie to the backyard where she found him doing it again.

Just as Mother was holding Clarice over the tub with one hand while rinsing her with the other, Hattie came in brandishing a bloody kitchen knife to announce that Reggie wouldn't ever play with himself again.

Mother dropped Clarice; ran to the garage picking up Reggie en route; backed out of the garage; and drove to the Doctor's office as fast as she dared.

Reggie bled to death on the way to the Doctor's office. When she returned home, Mother found Hattie dead in the driveway from having been run over. Only then did Mother remember Clarice, who was found drowned in the tub.

Talk about a hectic day . . .

Three variations on a grisly theme, each more detailed and "literary" in its style than the one before. The first was scrawled—in red ink on a sheet torn from a notebook—by my Salt Lake City friend and former student Sue Wolfe. The second, also handwritten, was sent to me by Marika Langton of Surrey, British Columbia, in 1990, who asked, "Does this sound like an urban legend to you?" The third variation, complete with names for the children, was carefully typewritten and sent in 1988 by Don E. Holt of Mobile, Alabama, who was responding to an urban legends column I had written that had appeared in the Mobile Press; *he remembered that it was told as a warning story but was not necessarily believed in.*

"Attempted Abductions"

This story arose about one year ago in Portogruaro [Italy] and is still taken very seriously by all the people in the area. Portogruaro is located about midway on the highway from Venice to Trieste, about fifty miles from the Slovenian border.

An enormous (by local standards) commercial center having been built close to the highway, free bus transportation is offered to prospective Yugoslav/Slovenian buyers. A certain number of Gypsies regularly come in among them.

A lady places her little child on a shopping trolley of the food market, before filling this one and three more with food she intends to buy. When queuing at the cashier's stand, she suddenly realizes that the child is gone.

Alarm—police—all exits closed and guarded!

After a two hours search, a smart female agent, remarking something odd in the walk of a plump Gypsy woman, immediately stops her and lifts her skirt, finding the child under there, packed in a shopping bag.

• • •

I was told this story last week in Islington, London. The person who told it to me believed it all; she swore it was true.

A woman friend of the estranged wife of an associate of hers was shopping in a mega store of Sainsbury's (a major UK food retailing chain) with her infant daughter. The store was in the suburbs; she couldn't remember where, but "somewhere like Harlow."

The woman was always careful with her daughter, but as she stretched to take a packet from a high shelf, she momentarily took her eyes off her. When she turned to put the carton in the shopping trolley the child had disappeared. Although she was a professional woman, always in control, she snapped and began to scream hysterically that her daughter had been stolen.

The security staff immediately closed all exits from the supermarket. After a careful search, the girl was found ten minutes later in a lavatory: in that short time her clothes had been completely changed and her hair dyed a different colour. The kidnapper was not caught, although, as I was told as an addendum to the story, there is a gang of people who do this.

• • •

Friends of a friend went to Disney World in Florida with their small daughter. They were told to be wary of kidnappers down there and not to let their child out of their sight. So when the mother went to the bathroom she took the child in with her while the father waited outside for the child to come out. While the mother was in the toilet and the child walking from the booth to the door, she disappeared.

The couple immediately notified security. The Disney World Security Department was accustomed to these occurrences and immediately closed all the gates except one, to let people depart the park. They told the parents to watch all the people who went out and to look at the faces of the children, not their clothing or hair color. Sure enough! The couple identified their child being taken out of the gate—the kidnappers had dyed her hair a different color and changed her clothes in the fifteen minutes she had been missing!

How's that for a hairy story?

• • •

Another friend some years ago told me how her daughter was shopping at Price Club and while her head was buried into the blouses looking for her size and her other hand rested on the shopping cart with her toddler in it. When she pulled out of the rack only to find her child gone! She was smart and yelled FIRE! then started making damage which attracted security officers. She told them the story, they quickly locked down the doors and searched for her child. Very lucky woman! They found her toddler already drugged in the back room, two teens were painting his hair black. All this took place in minutes! The teens were getting $10,000 for this blond blue eyed kid. On the market he would have sold for $25,000.

• • •

TRUE STORY:
Even if you do not have little kids, pass this one on to everyone you can think of. You never know who you might save by sending this e-mail!
Please take the time and forward this to any friend who has children & grandchildren!
I wanted to share something that happened today while shopping at Sam's Club.
A mother was leaning over looking for meat and turned around to find her 4yr. Old daughter was missing. I was standing there right beside her, and she was calling her daughter Katie with no luck.
I asked a man who worked at Sam's to announce it over the loud speaker for Katie. He did, and let me say, he immediately walked right past me when I asked and went to a pole where there was a phone. He made an announcement for all the doors and gates to be locked, a code something.
So they locked all the doors at once. This took all of 3 minutes after I asked the guy to do this. They found the little girl 5 minutes later in a bathroom stall. Her head was half shaved, and she was dressed in her underwear with a bag of clothes, a razor, and wig sitting on the floor beside her to make her look different.Whoever this person was, took the little girl, brought her into the bathroom, shaved half her head, and undressed her in a matter of less than 10 minutes.
This makes me shake to no end.Please keep a close eye on your kids when in big places where it's easy for you to get separated. It only took a few minutes to do all of this!
At another 5 minutes and she would have been out the door. I am

still in shock that some sick person could do this, let alone in a matter of minutes.

The days are over when our little ones could run rampant all over the place and nothing worse would happen to them.

The little girl is fine. Thank god for fast workers who didn't take any chances.

BE SURE TO FORWARD THIS TO EVERYONE, SO THEY KNOW JUST HOW SICK PEOPLE ARE OUT THERE!!!

(This happened at the Sam's Wholesale Club in Omaha, Nebraska.)

Variations on a theme. I slightly revised the English of the first version, which was sent to me from Italy in July 1992. The London version was sent by Jon King of Stoke Newington, England, in November 1992. The third came in a letter from Terry Parmelee of Washington, D.C., in October 1992. Fourth is a verbatim quotation of a paragraph from a newsletter dated spring 1997 and written by a radical feminist Wiccan author; the copy of the newsletter was sent to me by John J. Kane, director of "NH Skeptics" of Stratham, New Hampshire. Finally, I quote verbatim from an e-mail forwarded to me by several people in September 2002.

"Mutilated Little Boys"

I heard a story, I believe about ten years ago, it would be about 1965—I was eighteen then—about a little white boy who had gone shopping with his mother in K-Mart, and he had to urinate. So, for the first time the mother decided to let him go in by himself to use the men's washroom, rather than going into the women's with her. He was in there an exceptionally long amount of time, and she got worried and asked some gentlemen to step in and see what the problem was, if there was a problem.

And they found the little boy laying in a pool of blood with his penis cut off. Subsequently they found three little black boys walking through the store with a bloody penis in their pocket. As it turned out, they had cut the little white boy's penis off as an orientation, a method of getting into a gang that they wanted to belong to. And to get into the gang they had to cut the penis off a white boy, which they did do.

• • •

This was told to me by a good friend who heard it from a coworker who heard it from a friend or relative on the eastern end of Long Island, where it supposedly took place.

It seems a mother and her five- or six-year-old son were shopping in a big department store like Gimbels. The little boy had to go to the bathroom, and the mother wanted to take him to the ladies' room. However, the boy insisted he was old enough to go into the men's room. Finally the mother gave in, told him to hurry and she'd wait outside the door. Time goes by and he doesn't come out. The mother is becoming nervous and asks a middle-aged man who was going in to the men's room to check on him. Maybe he just needed help with his zipper. The man goes in and screams. Now the mother is in terror, dashes in herself. There is her son lying on the floor bleeding to death because someone had cut off his penis.

When my friend told the story she was so distraught she could hardly get the words out. The coworker who had told her had cried all day at work. . . .

• • •

This story is currently making the rounds in the Dallas/Fort Worth metroplex.

A mother and her eight-year-old boy were at Redbird mall shopping. The boy had to go to the bathroom, so the mother took him to one of the public restrooms and waited outside. Some other teenaged boys were also in the bathroom and were loud and boisterous. The mother waited and waited, the boy didn't come out. The teenagers left together, laughing. The boy still didn't come out. Finally, the mother went into the bathroom and found the boy in a pool of blood; the teenagers had cut his penis off.

More variations on a theme. The first version is from Richard M. Dorson, Land of the Millrats *(Cambridge, Mass.: Harvard University Press, 1981), p. 228, as told by a man in Gary, Indiana. The second is from a 1982 letter from Maureen Aguis-Scheeler of Wharton, New Jersey. The Dallas/Fort Worth version came from Dr. Rosemary E. Detweiler in a letter dated December 23, 1992.*

"The Hammered Child"

February 3, 1986
Dear Sirs:

Currently there is a six-year-old little girl in Primary Children's Hospital with no hands.

She apparently took a hammer to the family car and to punish her her father took the same hammer to her hands. By the time they got her to the hospital she had lost two fingers (they fell off) and then her blood vessels, bone, and nerves were so badly damaged that they had to amputate both hands.

The mother will not press charges because "he was in charge of discipline," and the hospital is being forced to return this child to these two crazy people.

For God's sake, can't the media do something.

I can't sign this because I'm only a private citizen and not supposed to know about this. Please do something.

Verbatim copy of a typewritten letter, evidently based on word-of-mouth rumors, received by several Salt Lake City news media and given to me by a local television reporter who checked out the story with law enforcement officials and with the named hospital. There was no such child, no such crime, and no cover-up. Typical urban legend motifs included are the supposed legal helplessness of a wronged person and the alleged suppression of damaging information by authorities.

"Pencils as Deadly Weapons"

Tuesday 21st May 1991

. . . I feel that I must bring to light one of the most gruesome and bizzare urban legends which I have come across.

I am a boy of fourteen at Oundle School, a top English boarding school in the picture-postcard town of Oundle in the countryside of Northamptonshire. I have known this story to be circulating for several years, so I am not sure how old it is.

It concerns a girl doing her A-Level exam (taken at eighteen). Having finished one of her exams and whilst still in the examination room, the results of one of her other exams is handed to her on a sheet of paper. She reads the paper, and discovers that in her last, and most important exam, she has failed miserably. She now can never get a good job and her parents will think that she is a failure. There and then she decides to commit suicide.

She takes two pencils and pushes them as far up her nostrils as they will go. She then (wait for it!) brings her head crashing down upon the desk. The pencils go through her skull and into her brain, killing her.

This is not the end of the story: there is a final twist. After checking the girl's results, the examiners discover that her marks have been mixed up, and that she has in fact, passed her exam!

Yours faithfully,
Rowland Byass

From a letter sent in response to having read one of my urban legend books.

ACCIDENTS

"Accidents will happen," the proverb says, and that's scary enough by itself. But when you hear about virtually the same grisly accidents happening over and over again, in many different times and places, that's super scary, until you realize that you may just be hearing another kind of urban horror legend—the story of the gory, often fatal, mishap that never occurred.

The first four accounts in this chapter are a case in point. All four stories (and there are many more versions) describe a person trapped in some kind of huge industrial equipment in such a way that either moving or restarting the equipment would be fatal; doing nothing also dooms the victim to certain death. Invariably in this well-known legend the hapless worker remains conscious until his death and requests a last meeting with his family, with whom he is then united, either in person or via a radio or telephone hookup. His last words are usually overheard by his horrified coworkers. Sometimes this kind of accident story is known as "The Last Kiss," focusing on the victim's last wish.

Another typical feature of this type of legend that is hardly likely in real life is that the victim remains cool and collected, despite his fate, sometimes smoking one last cigarette before personally giving the order to restart the machinery and snuff out his life.

Some contexts in which versions of the "Last Kiss" story are retold are suggested by our four texts. In the first example we eavesdrop on workers talking it over at a Midwestern steel mill; they are convinced that the incident did occur, although none of them actually witnessed it. In the other versions a coworker or a supervisor tells the story as a warning lesson to new members of the group. In all tellings, certain details of the accident are furnished (how it happened, exactly how he was trapped, even the specific length of time he suffered before dying), while other aspects, such as when and where the accident occurred, remain vague.

Despite the gory details and tragic outcome of such stories, some urban legends about accidents manage to sustain a humorous style. For example, in another story about getting caught in factory machinery, an old Swedish worker loses a finger while operating a giant buzz saw; asked how that could happen, the worker supposedly said something like, "Vell, I vas yust sawing like this and . . . voops, der goes annuder von!" (Feel free to retell this as a story about Norwegians, Poles, Italians, Irish, or any other nationality or ethnicity appropriate to your audience.)

It may seem hard to make a joke about the "Last Kiss" scenario, but the Canadian singer and songwriter Norman Walker has managed to do so. In his song "Interchange Two Phases," Walker describes "Johnny" working at the gravel pit who "slipped and fell and got pulled into the crusher machine." Thinking him doomed (for that's how the legend goes!), and assuming he was raving incoherently, his coworkers ignored Johnny's plea to:

Interchange two phases. . . .

It can be red, black or blue.
Interchange just any two.

Walker drew on his knowledge of how electrical engines work to have Johnny plead for his partners to reverse the wiring, thus backing up the motor and releasing him alive from the deathtrap. But with his girlfriend, Mary Lou, looking on, the others disregard this information, even though "He knew a three phase induction / motor was easy to reverse." So instead of being saved, Johnny dies:

> They turned to the crusher machine
> Turned it on and without a scream
> They mixed Johnny with the gravel on the other end.
> Now he's part of highway 105
> The road to Mary Lou's he used to drive.

Welding, to many people, is regarded as an especially dangerous kind of work, as demonstrated by two very common horror ULs included here. Both stories involve the interaction of welding sparks, or "microwaves," with other devices, namely contact lenses and butane lighters. Both warnings are typically circulated in typescript form, usually with spelling and punctuation errors, and both include spurious details, such as the mention of microwaves (from welding?!) or the description of the power of a tiny lighter exploding with "the same amount of force . . . as there is in three sticks of dynamite." It does not seem to detract from the popularity or the credibility of either story that both have been debunked repeatedly by safety officials, technical writers, and (last but not least) folklorists.

Accidents on the home front, not just at work, are the subject of urban legends, one of the most persistent being a bizarre story about a man (or men) cutting off his fingertips while trying to use a power mower to trim a hedge. A standard featured of this story is the account of a product-liability lawsuit against the mower manufacturer that succeeded in winning the victim, however stupid his actions, a large financial settlement. Again, debunkings have failed to suppress the story. Way back in the October 31, 1977, issue of *Advertising Age* this story was dismissed as apocryphal in an article that opened like this:

> That legendary product liability case in which a man picked up his lawn mower to trim a hedge, was injured and successfully sued the manufacturer may be just that—a legend.
>
> There is no evidence that the incident ever happened.

A collection of modern accident legends would not be complete without a couple of versions of the story about a scuba diver found up a tree in a burned-out area. The marine biologist who sent me the first quoted version of this contemporary classic provided a detailed analysis of its impossibility along the same lines as debunkings provided by divers, firefighters, and aircraft manufacturers. But the biologist's report also provides evidence about how such a story gets circulated and believed: two of her informants mentioned broadcasting and e-mail as ways they had heard the story, and my second example here, reprinted from a Los Angeles newspaper, confirms the power of these media as legend conduits and adds a third—print media.

"Caught in the Couplers"

Mike: Out in the yard, outside the fab shop at Bethlehem, there was a guy that was switching cars. And the engineer thought he got the signal to move the cars back, and this guy was in the middle of two cars; and he was crushed by the couplers, the couplers just closed in on him, but he was still alive when that happened. And this guy eventually died; 'cause everything in the middle was just squished.

Ben: You're working out there with guys that are drunk, engineers especially. And if they move, you got to work fast. There are certain ways you have to open up knuckles and drawbars of railroad car couplings by your hands. And you have to walk between train cars a lot of times. And you're supposed to make sure that nothing's coming either way. If you're working—sometimes you've got a busted pin, and you're changing a knuckle or something—you're standing right there in between them damn cars. You're supposed to get twenty foot of space, but I'll tell you something, you're lucky if you get twenty foot, 'cause things are so damn crowded.

So the guy is in there in between the cars, working. And this hogger wasn't drunk, but the brake slipped. And the car rolled back and coupled this guy up, coupled him right in the middle. It didn't really cut through him because it's very blunt. It just coupled him. So they got a hold of the cops and the ambulances, and everybody come over to where he was.

And the guy knew he was dead, and everybody knew he was dead. But his last wish is that he could talk to his family. Well, we couldn't get him to a phone before he died. So what they did is they hooked a phone through a radio. But unfortunately that radio went to all the radios in the mill, and all the trains through our radios. Everybody heard it. They cleared the lines, just telling us about the trainman who got caught between the couplings and was calling his wife on the radio. So the only way he could talk to his family was to talk to the radio and connect it to this phone line. And so everybody stopped all work; everybody stopped, man. And a lot of guys got off the train. But there was an outside speaker; no matter where you went, you still heard it. And the guy just got on the phone and weeped; it shook everybody up. Guys went home sick, almost the whole damn crew. And that's over two hundred guys on that particular shift. The yardmasters let 'em all go. So anyhow, he had to explain to his family the condition he was in. I guess about thirty minutes or so.

Paul: He lived that long?

Ben: He lived longer than that. They figured in his condition that he would live, before he would lapse into a coma, about sixteen hours.

Paul: How long did they have him that way?

Ben: He had been that way three and a half hours before they could get the hook-up of the telephone. And by that time he had enough of his shit together where he could rap to his family. So he explained to his family, I guess about thirty minutes or so.

Paul: And then, finally, he just said: "Go ahead and pull the car."

Ben: Well, yeah. After he got done talking and whatever, and said his goodbye and all this good stuff, he handed them back the radio. 'Cause he still had movement in his body—part of it anyhow. Maybe the spine was severed. He had movement in the upper half. And they wrapped sheets around his body. They pulled the pin [makes a slapping sound], and he said goodbye. That was it, you're dead. Just like that. He exploded. Because of the pressure.

I didn't hear him myself. I'm glad I didn't. I wasn't working switchman then. But my father told me about it. This was in seventy-two, early seventy-two, just about when we got our hand radios in. That's the last major death—well, I can't say the last, but that's the first and last time they did anything like that.

• • •

In 1979 I was told a story by a coworker who was deadly serious. It has always bothered me as it is obviously medically impossible, but the person who told me believed it completely.

The tale goes that one night as a switchman was working in the yard in Kansas (or someplace) he was coupled between two rail cars—completely through his midsection. This dreadful accident did not kill the man immediately, but others at the scene knew that the only way to exctricate him from his gruesome predicament was to uncouple the cars. Everyone knew the man would bleed to death when this was done.

The railroad worker had never lost consciousness and when told of his imminent demise requested his wife and children be brought to his side. After the family hurried to the scene of the accident and tearful last good-byes were said, railroad officials reluctantly uncoupled the two cars.

. . . the man soon bled to death, but at least he had a last moment with his family.

The teller insisted it actually happened on our railroad (the former Missouri Pacific). He didn't know exactly where it occurred or the names of the people involved, just that it really did happen. I have heard this story repeated to new employees by various people.

The first version is a tape-recorded conversation made in 1975 or '76 with three young steel-mill workers in the heavily industrialized Calumet region of northwest Indiana and published in Richard M. Dorson's Land of the Millrats *(Cambridge, Mass.: Harvard University Press, 1981), pp. 63–64. The second was sent to me in 1990 by Elisa E. Tubbs, assistant to the vice president of the Union Pacific Railroad Company's office in Baton Rouge, Louisiana.*

"The Crushed Soldier"

I've heard [this story] expressed several different ways:

A soldier is driving a Jeep which suddenly overturns and crushes the man at the waist so that he is essentially "cut in two." Because the pinning effectively isolates the upper torso from the lower body, the man remains fully conscious without pain and fully conversant with his predicament. As others are about to free him he orders them to wait long enough for him to have one last cigarette. After he has concluded his smoking, he gives the signal to lift the Jeep, whereupon he instantly expires.

Variants of this [I have heard] are a railroad worker trapped under an overturned boxcar and an elevator maintenance worker trapped between the car and the floor landing.

• • •

❡ heard this while in the army, stationed in West Germany during 1985–89. I served with Third Brigade Forward, First Infantry Division, garrisoned in the Stuttgart area of southern Germany. There's a big maneuver and live-fire training area up towards Frankfurt called Grafenwohr. We went there three to four times a year, two weeks at a time for a lot of miserable field training.

The army utilizes a lot of heavy, dangerous equipment. Well, there was a platoon sergeant, one day, while we were at Graf, who was giving the armored personnel carrier (APC) drivers in my outfit a safety briefing. With great sobriety he launched into this story concerning a private who drove his APC parallel with the slope of a hill.

The slope was too steep, and the APC rolled over and the track commander (TC) was thrown from the hatch that he was standing half out of. The two-plus-ton APC came to rest laying upside down on top of the TC's legs and lower abdomen. The combat medics could do nothing for the nearly severed-at-the-middle TC. The field surgeon arrived, examined the soldier, and pronounced that nothing could be done to save him. The surgeon explained that when the APC was lifted off the soldier, he would die almost immediately of a massive hemorrhage. Conversely, if it wasn't lifted off, he would die in an hour or so due to numerous internal injuries.

At this point the field commander, a general, ordered a field telephone to be patched into the civilian phone network so that the soldier's wife could be reached from the accident site. While the phone was being set up, heavy recovery vehicles and their crews arrived and busied themselves getting ready to lift the APC back over onto its tracks. Amazingly, the half-crushed soldier was conscious and alert throughout all of this!

The phone connection was made and the dying soldier was

given the receiver. He explained to his stunned wife that an APC was lying on top of his guts, and he was going to die very soon; he said he loved her very much and wished her the best. With this the phone was disconnected, the general gave the order to right the APC, and the APC was lifted off. The soldier died within seconds as his blood, no longer trapped by the weight of the APC, gushed from his lower half.

The safety sergeant concluded, "You drivers be damn careful how you drive those things." We, of course, were awed by this grisly tale.

The first version was sent to me in 1990 by Harvey M. Haeberle of Mattawan, Michigan. The second came to me in 1994 from Steve Rimney of Medical Lake, Washington.

"Welded Contact Lenses"

TO: All Industrial Education Teachers
FROM: [name deleted]
DATE: March 29, 1983
SUBJECT: Eye Safety

NOTICE******NOTICE******NOTICE******NOTICE
The following information has been called to my attention regarding wearing contact eye lenses and <u>accidental electrical arc flashes</u>. Read and discuss with your students and take immediate action.

"The probability of this occuring is growing every day with the vast reduction in cost and availability of contact lenses. It is very possible you may not be aware of who does wear such lenses to work.

Two recent incidents have uncovered a previously unknown phenomenon of serious gravity.

At Duquesne Electric, a worker threw an electrical power switch into closed position which produced a short-lived sparking. An employee, at UPS, flipped open the colored lens of his welding goggles to better position the welding rod. He inadvertently struck the metal to be welded, producing an arc.

Both men were wearing contact lenses. On returning home from work, they removed the contacts and the cornea of the eye was removed along with the lens. Result: <u>PERMANENT BLINDNESS!</u>

The electric arc generates microwaves that instantly dry up the fluid between the eye and the lens, causing the cornea to be bonded to the lens. This trauma is painless and the operator never knows an injury has occurred until removing the contacts.

As this phenomenon was unknown, no Federal or State safety and health agency has regulations on this matter but they are pursuing the investigation zealously and will respond according to findings.

At this juncture there appears to be two enforcement options. Until Federal and State standards are adopted, prohibit all contact-wearing personnel, who are potentially subject to an electrical sparking environment, from wearing this mode of corrective lenses or mandate that dark green protective eyewear be consistently used."

A verbatim copy of a memo printed on the letterhead of the Granite School District of Salt Lake City, Utah. On the original, all underlinings

were inserted by hand and the word "Important!" was written in the
left-hand margin. The words "IMMEDIATE ACTION REQUESTED"
were stamped on a diagonal across the top. This widely circulated bogus
warning is especially long-lived; in late 2001 a version of it was circulated to offshore oil and gas installations in the North Sea, identified as a
reprint from an Australian newspaper.

"Exploding Butane Lighters"

In recent months, the Union-Pacific Railroad has had two
fatal accidents caused by butane lighters. These accidents
occurred in welding areas when an employee was welding
with a butane lighter in his pocket. A spark from the welding
landed on the lighter, burned through, exposing the fluid,
which exploded. One lighter was in a shirt pocket and killed
the individual instantly. The other lighter was in the pants
pocket and caused an amputation. The man later died.

It is estimated that there is the same amount of force in a
butane lighter when it explodes as there is in three sticks of
dynamite. Please warn anyone using these lighters of the
potential hazard. Most folks don't realize that they are walking around with the equivalent of three sticks of dynamite in
their pocket.

A verbatim example from 1980 of a story that was widely distributed in
the form of memos, fliers, handouts, and published articles during the
late 1970s and early 1980s.

"Lawn-Mower Accidents"

A man finishes mowing his lawn, and, surveying his hedges, he decides they need trimming. Too lazy to get out his hedge trimmer, he decides to save time and effort, so he beckons his neighbor to give him a hand using the power mower instead. Each man grabs the bottom of the mower, then straddles the hedge as they plan to walk along trimming it. Sure enough, both guys get their fingertips chopped off, and they decide to sue the company for not having a safety warning in the mower manual about hedge cutting. The case goes to court, and the jury agrees with the plaintiffs, who receive a lucrative settlement.

• • •

O ther uses may emerge for the product beyond those planned by the design team. Although "form follows function" is a familiar phrase, function can also follow form.

A homeowner doing repairs may use a crescent wrench to push in a light nail. . . . An 18-inch-high flat-topped wall can be used as a bench despite signs saying it is a flower retainer.

While these examples are harmless, others can be dangerous. For instance, a lawnmower company was sued by a user who picked up the mower to use as a hedge trimmer and proceeded to cut several of his fingers. The user's lawyers argued that nothing told the user the whirling blades were not to be used to cut hedges.

The first version of this common story is a generic retelling, as I have heard it many times. The second version is an example of the same story used as a cautionary tale in an editorial published in Machine Design *on November 9, 1989; this version was later identified as apocryphal in a letter to the editor published in the January 11, 1990, issue of the same publication.*

"Up a Tree"

I heard this story first from a college student, then—within two days—I heard it independently from two colleagues who were repeating it as if it were true. One heard it from "someone who heard it on the news," and the other "saw this on e-mail":

Recently some people were walking in the Santa Monica mountains above Malibu, in an area that had burned in the wildfires of 1993. In the middle of nowhere, in a wooded area, they came across the body of a human being. It was fully outfitted for diving, with wet suit, mask, regulator, tank of air, and swim fins. How had he gotten there? What was he doing high in the mountains, several miles inland?

It was found that he had died of massive internal injuries. The only logical explanation that they could come up with was that this must have occurred during the raging fires. Giant firefighting helicopters had been brought in, and these flew over the ocean, scooping up water in huge buckets carried by ropes. Then they flew up to the hills and dropped the water onto the fires. The unfortunate person had been diving in the ocean just at this time, and he was unwittingly scooped up by one of these buckets and dropped to a horrible death.

● ● ●

You think the bends is painful for divers . . .

Radio station KFWB-AM (980) noticed a blurb on the Internet that claimed that "fire authorities in California" had found the body of a scuba diver in a burnt section of a forest.

The diver, "complete with a dive tank, flippers and face-mask," supposedly was found 12 miles from the ocean. And an examination revealed that the victim had died "not from burns but from massive internal injuries."

The Internet account said that it was later determined that the diver had been in the ocean the day of the fire and was apparently scooped up by one of a fleet of helicopters "with very large buckets. The buckets were dropped into the ocean for rapid filling, then flown to the forest fire and emptied."

Hence the massive internal injuries.

KFWB checked with the state Department of Forestry and was informed that the story was a hoax—one that crops up every year or so.

Put it in your file of urban folk tales.

The first report was sent to me in June 1996 by Karen Martin, a marine biologist at Pepperdine University in Malibu, California. The second account is from an undated clipping from the Los Angeles Times *sent to me in August 1996 by Robert Goldfarb of Studio City, California. Taken together, these two versions of an often-repeated story show oral tradition, broadcasting, print media, and the Internet all participating in the circulation of a scary urban legend.*

"Boil on Troubled Waters"

In an e-mail from England dated 3/23/00:

A safety and security officer in Trinidad reported that a 26 year old man was using a microwave oven to heat some water to make a cup of instant coffee, something he had done many times before. Having set the microwave to boil the water, he removed the cup immediately [after] the microwave had switched itself off. As he looked into the cup he noted that the water was not boiling; how-ever, it suddenly erupted into his face due to the build up of energy caused by the boiling process. His face was badly blis-tered with 1st and 2nd degree burns which may leave scarring and also the partial loss of sight in one eye.

This warning was circulated in a health and safety newsletter at the University of Westminster, London, and it was e-mailed to me from there; many other versions, which repeat many of the same details, have circu-lated on the Internet in various forms. The title used above—a parody of the saying about pouring oil on troubled waters—comes from the urban legend Web site www.snopes.com, where this story is marked "status undetermined," i.e., is it legend or fact? In a Scripps Howard News Service article by Erin Shaw released to newspapers on February 8, 2000, the exploding-water story is described as "suspended between urban leg-end and partial truth." Shaw, who writes for the Birmingham (Alabama) Post-Herald, *quotes several authorities who validated some aspects of the process described but expressed serious doubts about the whole incident; I was e-mailed her article by my brother-in-law William F. Ast III, who writes for the* Benton Harbor/St. Joseph (Michigan) Herald Palladium.

CRIMINAL INTENT

Sorting scary urban legends into logical categories—like Infestation, Accidents, or Crime—is problematic at best. After all, the various hook men, slashers, smugglers, abductors, hit-and-run drivers, negligent parents, thieves, etc. portrayed in the legends of earlier chapters are all criminal types, as are also, in a sense, the companies that are said to sell dangerous or contaminated products, or the people who play fatal pranks. But we really can't put all the scary stories into just one or two categories, which leaves us, frankly, with several pretty solid groupings and quite a few leftovers, as with this chapter of chillers about assorted lurking creeps with criminal intent.

Even so, there are some other similarities among these stories about crime. For example, the first three sets of legends all involve severed or burned fingers or hands, and all three of them also have prototypes in European legends or folktales. "The Choking Doberman," featuring a *bitten*-off finger, derives from a Welsh legend about Prince Llewellyn and his dog Gelert, which in turn developed out of Middle Eastern fables concerning other faithful but misunderstood pets. Likewise, "The Robber Who Was Hurt" is a transformation of an old European supernatural legend called "The Witch Who Was Hurt," while all the various modern stories about fingers and hands cut off in order to steal rings contain elements of an older folktale called "The Clever Maid at Home Kills the Robbers."

Historical and comparative notes do not make the stories any scarier; perhaps they make them less so. What enhances their chilling effect are statements by modern storytellers such as "This is really true . . . " or "It happened right over in [fill in the place] . . . " or "My mother was telling me about another woman she knows who. . . . " Such localized and personalized tellings of urban crime legends by a claimed friend of a friend of the actual victim bring crime statistics and news stories right down to the level of the individual, who may feel as if he or she is the next possible victim. Hundreds of fragmentary rumors and legends may circulate about supposed crime waves in a region, and occasionally a folklore collector may construct a more coherent narrative from these bits and pieces, as in this summary account titled "The Maniac on the Underground" written by an English folklorist:

> There is a Maniac on the London Underground. His identity is of course unknown—likewise, his physical appearance is vague; however, he is a true homicidal or psychopathic maniac.
>
> The Maniac lurks on crowded station platforms, positioning himself behind a chosen victim who is close to the platform edge. As the train rushes out of the tunnel and into the station, the Maniac, with fiendish timing, imparts a short, sharp shove to the victim's back, causing that unfortunate to fall onto the rails and beneath the oncoming train. In the ensuing confusion and terror, the Maniac melts away in the crowds and is never detected nor captured. (Michael

Goss, "The Halifax Slasher and Other 'Urban Maniac'
Tales," in *Perspectives on Contemporary Legend V: A Nest of
Vipers*, ed. Gillian Bennett and Paul Smith [Sheffield,
England: Academic Press, 1990], p. 90.)

It seldom seems to lessen people's fear of such attacks that
few, if any, actual crimes of this kind are ever reported in the
media. Similarly, psychics are notoriously "off " in most of
their predictions, yet rumor patterns like the "Campus Murder
Scares" detailed below recur year after year, attributed to popular psychics, without any such crimes ever actually occurring. Some people rationalize this by claiming that the
warnings scared away the criminals, while others point to differently detailed actual campus killings as evidence that such
crimes really do happen. So why didn't the psychics anticipate that the criminals would be scared off or visualize the
crimes correctly? Much the same lack of evidence for
rumored crimes could be proved by reviewing the annual
scares surrounding supposed tampering with Halloween
treats or the recurring fantasy stories about clowns in black
vans trying to kidnap children. The "Lights Out!" bogus warnings are yet another example of a frightening, yet undocu-
mented, threat of random violence against innocent citizens.
"You just can't be too careful" is the message in all of these
legends. Besides, as I phrased it elsewhere, "The truth never
stands in the way of a good story."
    The wide circulation of legends about criminal intent is
suggested in this chapter by their being versions quoted across
many years from scattered American cities as well as from
several foreign locales. The variations of detail—typical of
folklore—are as common in the crime stories as in any others.
In general, as legends are repeated, there is a tendency to
update details: a witch becomes a robber; a hot iron substi-
tutes for a fireplace poker; a maid alone at home becomes a

woman trying on clothes in a mall store's dressing room; and the cited "facts" of the supposed criminal assaults in the crime legends include modern elements such as the layout of a contemporary college campus, the use of headlight high beams on an automobile, or specifically a *Carousel* slide projector showing the "Indecent Exposure" slides, a detail that has been updated in recent versions to a video camcorder and VCR. And then we get the contemporary thieves who instead of trying to pick your pocket simply steal directly from your account via the bank's ATM.

To balance the legends about assailants getting away with crimes, I include a couple of stories here in which the crooks get what they deserve, or receive what the storytellers regard as "justice" or even "poetic justice." That kind of neat plot twist is further evidence that we are dealing with folklore rather than straightforward facts. It reminds me of what the *Akron (Ohio) Beacon Journal* (April 26, 1996) added as a sidebar to a fine report on crime legends by writer Kerry Coughlin titled "Playing Cops 'n' Rumors." Under the heading "Myth Clues," the paper listed various clues to detect an urban myth (it should be urban *legend*, but nobody's perfect). As Coughlin advised, a story is likely to be fictitious if

- the source is a friend of a friend;
- the anecdote is accompanied by the claim that it's true;
- the story comes with a warning;
- there's a twist at the end;
- in the moral to the story, a person pays for his or her sins.

I couldn't have said it better myself.

"The Choking Doberman"

(**M**y informant, a single woman, was reluctant at first to relate the story, wanting to leave out the racial element, but I asked her to tell the story as she heard it from a woman who came to her place of employment, the Slidell [Louisiana] Humane Society.)

This is supposed to be a true story that happened in Metairie. She said that the woman had gotten a Doberman Pinscher, was frightened of living alone, and she left it in the apartment, and she went to work. This is the first day she had the dog, OK? And she came back from work. She went in, and she couldn't find the dog. So she called the dog, and it didn't come. So, finally, she looked all over the house, and she went into the bedroom, and there was the dog, and it was choking.

So she quick called the veterinarian, and he was just about to close. So he says, "Put the dog in the car and come down here right away, if it's choking." So she did. And so, the dog was still choking [hands around throat—cough, cough, cough] and so he said, "I think you better leave it here overnight. You go on home before it gets any later. I'll go ahead and work on it."

So she went back on home, and when she entered, the phone was ringing when she got back to the apartment. And he said, "Leave your apartment immediately and call me back!" And she said, "What are you talking about? Who is this?" and he said, "This is Dr. So-and-so, the veterinarian." And he said, "GET OUT OF THAT APARTMENT. GO TO ANOTHER TELEPHONE. GO TO A NEIGHBOR OR FRIEND OR SOMETHING LIKE THAT." She said, "You must be out of your mind!" So he said, "Alright, if you won't leave any other way," he said, "would you like to know what was choking that dog? TWO BLACK FINGERS!"

And she panicked, and she dropped the phone and ran over to a neighbor and called him back, and said, "Alright, I'm over at the neighbors. Did you say two black fingers?"

"Yes," he said. "Call the cops."

So she called the cops. They searched the house. In her closet was a black dude. He had passed out from loss of blood. He was jammed way back up in the closet, and he was missing two fingers. He had gotten into that apartment and he was waiting for her, and they caught him.

And she said she'd never ever part with that dog.

Tape-recorded and transcribed by William D. Snyder of Slidell, Louisiana, in April 1982 for a folklore-class project at the University of New Orleans taught by Professor Ethelyn Orso, and sent to me in July 1982. Bracketed comments are the collector's; where I have used all capital letters, Mr. Snyder had simply noted "Emphasis."

"The Robber Who Was Hurt"

Told in Dublin:

There was this old lady, and evidently she was very, very . . . now, again, this is a true story. . . . Mrs. Barnwell knows this woman. And evidently she did the same thing every day. She was an old-age pensioner and she lived on her own. And she went out to Mass in the morning, did her bit of shopping, and then she came in and she set her fire and made her lunch and what have you.

And when she had all tidied up and everything, then it was always her habit that she would light the fire, put the screen around it, and she would go down as far as the chapel then and say her rosary. And then that was her outing for the day, and her neighbours and all whom she was very friendly with knew that this was her usual routine.

So anyway, off she went, and on her way down this day to the chapel as usual, she got cramps in her stomach. And she decided that she better not continue on, that she'd come back home. And she came back, put the key in the door, came in, and she thought she heard a noise down in the kitchen. And she went down, and she listened, and she could hear . . . like a sort of sawing noise, you know. And she just stood her ground, and she waited, and the next thing she saw the blade of a little . . . you know, a hack-saw blade, a little narrow blade coming in through a cut in the door. So she waited, and she looked, and the sawing kept continuing on. She couldn't see through the door who it was or anything. But she saw the sawing.

And back up she goes to the fire that she had already lit, as I said, puts the poker in it, and reddens the poker. And she came down. And just as your man cut the square . . . he was cutting a piece out around the lock for to put in his hand to open the door . . . and just as he put in his hand, she left the red poker on the back of his hand. And he fell back screaming outside of the door. And she could hear the person getting up and running away. So after about an hour and all, when everything was quiet, or half an hour, when she knew everything . . . that he was gone, and everything, she went out to call the woman next door to tell her what had happened. And one of the youngsters came out, and she called him and she says, "Is your mammy there?" And he says, "No, me mammy is gone to the shops." And she says, "Is your daddy there?" And he says, "No, me daddy is gone to the hospital. He got an awful bad burn on his hand."

You see, it was the man next door, that knew the time she would be out, and that she'd be out for a couple of hours, and he was evidently coming in to raid the place while she was out.

•   •   •

Told in Syracuse, New York:

This story was sent to me by a friend in Switzerland who had heard it from a friend in Syracuse, New York, who assured her that it was true.

A well-to-do widow, living alone, had a birthday coming up. Shortly before the date she received in the mail, anonymously, two tickets to a concert, and she asked a friend to go with her. All this was shared with a married friend who lived next door.

Just before the concert the friend backed out, and the widow decided to stay home. She didn't mention the change in plans to her next-door friend. That evening the widow was in the basement, ironing quietly. Suddenly she saw a hand reach under the curtains which were covering an open window. Without thinking, she thrust the hot iron onto the hand, which quickly withdrew. When she got over the shock, the widow ran next door to tell her married friend.

That woman was in a frenzy herself. "I can't talk now," she said, "I've got to take care of my husband. He just got a terrible burn on his hand!"

The Irish version was collected in 1980 by folklorist Éilís Ní Dhuibhne, who sent me a copy, which I quote verbatim except for omitting a few "anyway's" and "evidently's." The American version, which includes the free-tickets motif typically found in this country, was sent to me in 1987 by Patricia L. Hudelson of Cazenovia, New York.

"Cut-Off Fingers and Hands"

I heard about it about a year ago when I . . . started at my job at the card store in the mall. And some co-workers were talking about Christmastime and they told me that they heard about a woman who had gone shopping at Sears & Roebuck in the Plaza. And her husband had dropped her off, uh, maybe fifteen, twenty minutes before it was about to close. And she wanted to go in to pick up something she had seen earlier and she went in there and all the employees started to come out and the husband got a bit worried so he went and talked to a security guard and told them what was going on and they searched the dressing rooms. They found her on the floor and her ring was gone and her finger had been removed and she was unconscious.

• • •

My mother was telling me that another woman she knows said that a woman was going to the ladies' room in Filene's [Bargain] Basement. She entered the ladies' room, two women approached her, and asked her to take her, uhm she had a diamond ring on her finger, and they told her to take it off. She explained to them that she could not take the ring off because it was . . . stuck and they then struggled with her and at that point one of the girls pulled a knife, cut her finger, took the ring, and locked her in the bathroom and left her there.

And then later someone went back, went to go into the ladies' room and then found the woman there bleeding severely . . . also I knew, that it, was uhm, black females. After the incident, she [the teller's mother] was fearful because she goes shopping in downtown Boston. She went to the jewellers and she had her ring adjusted. So that, you know, 'cause what if she was in the same situation? She has arthritis, her fingers swell and she can't even move them . . . so she went to the jewellers and he had it adjusted so that it can be taken on and off.

• • •

As I heard it, a lady was sitting on a train. And this guy walked in and he had this trench coat on. He sat down and he was kind of nervous and jittery. So she noticed there was blood around one of his coat pockets. And it seemed like it was coming from there and his hand was in his pocket. So she went and got a cop. And I guess the police went over to the guy and frisked him and went through him or whatever. And come to find out there was a woman's finger in his pocket and it had a diamond on it.

• • •

A friend of mine said she had heard that a friend of a friend was on a bus in Newark, N.J. A shady looking man got on the bus with an overcoat on. Several of the other riders noticed this man had blood dripping from inside of his coat. One of the passengers alerted the bus driver who used some device on the bus to alert a passing police car that there was trouble on the bus. The police pulled over the bus and when they forced the man to open his coat, they found he was holding a hand which he had cut off of a victim in order to steal some rings.

The first three stories were collected in 1982 in Massachusetts by Eleanor Wachs and published in "The Mutilated Shopper at the Mall: A Legend of Urban Violence," in Perspectives on Contemporary Legend V: A Nest of Vipers, *ed. Gillian Bennett and Paul Smith (Sheffield, England: Academic Press, 1990), pp. 147, 156–58. The fourth story was sent to me by Maryann Bodayle of South Orange, New Jersey, in 1990.*

"Campus Murder Scares"

The 1988 Outbreak

Mass Murder Rumor Panics Area Students
Terror was struck into the hearts of many ONU [Ohio Northern University] students over the Halloween weekend, all because of a rumor that spread like wildfire.

It began with a simple report that a psychic on the Phil Donahue show—a creditable source, no?—predicted a mass murder would occur at a small college in northwestern Ohio. The college name would begin with an "O," and the campus would be very flat. All signs point to Ohio Northern. . . .

Someone heard that a mass murder would happen at either ONU, OSU-Lima, Kent State, or Bowling Green; someone else heard that it would happen in an X-shaped building.

Popular belief was that the murderer would appear at a masquerade party, dressed as Little Bo Peep. As a result, "Little Bo Peep," costumes were banned at many Halloween parties. . . .

• • •

Trick or Truth? Ghastly Rumor Obsesses College

Greg Walker will sleep in an upper bunk on the top floor of Founders Hall this weekend. If a mass murderer comes to the Slippery Rock University [Pennsylvania] campus this Halloween weekend, that will put him at the epicenter of the violence. . . .

Graduates told him they heard it four or five years ago. He has met students at other Pennsylvania colleges who say the rumor is about their college, not Slippery Rock.

The rumor always involves mass murders on certain college campuses about the time of Halloween.

Robert Dawson, director of university advancement at Slippery Rock, said he remembers the rumor encompassing Pennsylvania colleges as an undergraduate 24 years ago, and in some form every two or three years since. . . .

"It's bad this year," he [the university police chief] said. "A lot of people are going home for the weekend or sleeping away from the dorm. Freshman girls seem to be scared the most. Freshmen girls are petrified. . . . "

[One official] has heard anywhere from four to 13 dead. Always a psychic predicts it. . . . The college is named after the local town and it has a body of water running through it. . . . Rumor says the murders will occur at either the highest or lowest point on campus. . . . Doubters on the first floor [of Founders Hall] believe the mass murder will happen there, since they are at the lowest spot. But so do residents of the fifth floor, who heard eight people would be murdered. On the eighth floor, they heard five people would be murdered. . . .

The murderer has changed over the years, beginning with the lone mass murderer who was in vogue a few years ago.

Now the rumor includes a cult, sometimes religious and often satanic. . . .

Most versions of the rumor blame it on a television show—usually Phil Donahue's. . . . Others have attributed the rumor to Oprah Winfrey, Johnny Carson, Jeane Dixon, Sally Jesse Raphael, and the NBC Nightly News. . . .

• • •

Wild Rumors of Campus Massacre Run Amok at FSU

The Florida State University community was on full alert Monday night after reports—supposedly started by a psychic on the Oprah Winfrey show—that a knife-wielding maniac, perhaps dressed as Little Bo Peep, would slash his way through a sorority house or a dormitory. . . .

The rumor held that last week a psychic appeared on the talk show and announced that a massacre would occur at a major university south of the Georgia border. The university would have a cemetery next to it, and the massacre would happen in a U-shaped building.

There was also some speculation the murderer would be dressed up as Little Bo Peep. . . .

• • •

Holloween [sic] Rumors Give Some Meredith Hall Residents Scare

Nearly half of the women at Meredith Hall [Purdue University] spent Monday evening away from their rooms in response to rumors circulating [on] campus about Halloween killings.

"At first I just thought it was a rumor, but the more it was publicized . . . on the Phil Donahue show and my roommate's parents read the prediction in their hometown newspaper in Minnesota, I thought that there was a slight chance some psycho might feel this was his calling.

"So, just to be safe, I didn't spend the night in Meredith," Manjusha Sakore, a freshman in the Schools [*sic*] of Engineering, said.

Various versions of an ax murderer coming to kill 12 people in an X-shaped dorm on Halloween night have been circulating the campus for the past month.

The 1991 Outbreak

Oprah Show's Prophecy for BU a Fraud

Boston University deputy police chief Anne W. Verge said there is no basis to a rumor circulating on campus about a psychic who appeared on *The Oprah Winfrey Show* this week predicting there would be a "massacre" at BU.

Verge said BUPD received a call from an "adamant" woman who claimed she was a student at Brown University in Providence, R.I., saying that a friend who attends BU saw an episode of the talk-show where a psychic said there would be a massacre at either BU or Providence College.

The woman said the psychic alleged the incident would happen "on the weekend of [October] 25th and it would happen in an L-shaped building." . . .

• • •

Spooky Murder Rumor Is No Treat for Colleges

A false rumor about an impending tragedy has been sweeping campuses in the Northeast, panicking some students, eliciting phone calls from worried parents and causing administrators to issue statements reassuring students the rumor is not true.

Details of the rumor vary to fit the campus upon which it is being spread. But the gist is that a psychic has predicted on television that a disaster, massacre or murder will occur in the days around Halloween on a campus with particular characteristics.

At the University of Massachusetts, the rumor was of a

mass murder at a campus with a pond and a building named for President John F. Kennedy.

At other schools, the key features were an L-shaped dorm or a domed stadium or a dorm near a cemetery. . . .

The most commonly cited source is the "Oprah Winfrey Show," although some versions say it was Cable News Network or "A Current Affair." . . .

At the University of Massachusetts' Amherst campus, women living in Emerson and James dormitories were so frightened that between 70 and 100 of them met Thursday with John Luippold, the campus police chief. . . .

Donald Stewart, executive director of public relations for Wheaton College in Norton . . . said despite denials from the Winfrey show, "I have people look me in the eye and tell me they saw" such a show.

• • •

Rumors of Slayings Sweep New England Colleges

A frightening rumor about an impending mass murder is spreading across college campuses in the Northeast, prompting some schools to call meetings and issue statements to comfort worried students. . . . The rumor, which has been heard at no fewer than six colleges from New Hampshire to Connecticut, comes in several versions.

In one version, a psychic appearing on Oprah Winfrey's television show supposedly predicted that a massacre would occur on a New England campus sometime around Halloween. In another, the killings are said to have been predicted in the writings of Nostradamus, the 16th-century mystic. . . .

Excerpts from news reports; from 1988: "Mass Murder Rumor . . . ," from a story by Stephanie Hink in the Northern Review, *December 6; "Trick or Truth? . . . ," from a story by Dan Donovan in the* Pittsburgh Press,

October 28; "Wild Rumors . . . , " from a story by Gary Fineout in the Florida State University paper Flambeau, *sometime in November; "Holloween [sic] Rumors . . . ," from a story by Ramona Welty in the Purdue university paper* Exponent, *November 2; from 1991: "Oprah Show's Prophecy . . . ," from a story by Melanie DeCarolis in the* Boston University Daily Free Press, *October 11; "Spooky Murder Rumor . . . ," from a story by Jean Caldwell in the* Boston Globe, *October 28; "Rumors of Slayings . . . " from a widely reprinted AP wire story, October 29.*

"Lights Out!"

* READ *

Date: October 15, 1993
FROM: Pat Duffy, Manager, Safety Department
TO: All Employees and their Families

We were made aware of the following bulletin from the Norfolk Southern Police Department (Virginia): and have confirmed through the New Castle County and Wilmington Police Departments that similar events have occurred in Los Angeles, Chicago, and Baltimore. Please take the time to read the remainder of this memo and inform your family members and friends. This awareness and precaution is important for both drivers and passengers, whether at home or traveling on business or pleasure.

BULLETIN

!!! THERE IS A NEW GANG INITIATION !!!

"This new 'initiation' of 'MURDER' is brought about by Gang members driving around with their car lights off. When you flash your car lights to signal them that their lights are out, the Gang members take it literally as 'LIGHTS OUT', so they follow you to your destination and kill you!!! That's their initiation.

Two families have already fallen victim to this initiation ritual in the St. Louis and Chicago areas.

This information should be given widespread distribution on your respective territories and posted on all bulletin boards. Beware and inform your families and friends.

DO NOT FLASH YOUR CAR LIGHTS FOR ANYONE

The above information was furnished by the Illinois State Police Department

THIS IS NOT A JOKE!!!

• • •

[March 10, 1994] . . . I heard this from my husband who heard it on the radio. . . . It seems that a new gang initiation in Chicago is to drive around with your car headlights off. When another driver flashes the car without headlights, that car will turn around and follow the driver back to his house. As the driver leaves his car, the gang members then attack and kill the driver who flashed them.
    . . . About a month later, several of the women at work were discussing this story in the lunchroom. While no one knew of a firsthand account, everyone decided that with all the violence in the world today, it must be true. . . . [Some said that] the Chicago PD had circulated a confidential internal memo on the subject, and the police did not want the story publicized because it could hurt tourism.

• • •

[March 29, 1994] . . . I overheard my secretary warning her sister this afternoon that at night where she lives there apparently are cars full of Satan worshippers driving around without their headlights on. If you blink your lights at them they will shoot you, and if everybody in your car is not dead, they will back up and finish you off.

She was told about this by the driver of her van pool who heard it from a friend who saw a sign warning people about this in a store window. Nobody has been shot or has witnessed a shooting, but it is supposedly occurring in the Beaver Springs, Snyder County, area of central Pennsylvania. . . .

The first warning memo—actually a bogus *warning—is a verbatim copy of one of hundreds of nearly identical copies I received in 1993 and 1994, when the rumor was rampant, particularly as an e-mailed or faxed notice put on various organizational letterheads. Typical here are the awkward wording, the random punctuation, the use of capitalization—and sometimes handwritten additions—for emphasis, and the totally unverified references to supposed persons issuing the warning and to the places threatened by this supposed crime. The two dated comments documenting some local reactions to the warning are excerpted from two of hundreds of letters I received on the same subject; they came from Teresa Shattuck of Oak Park, Illinois, and Allen Taylor of New Cumberland, Pennsylvania.*

"Indecent Exposures"

Heard in Colorado:

This was told to me by an earnest young man who swears it happened recently to some friends of his parents.

An older couple took a long anticipated trip to Costa Rica,

and when they arrived they found to their dismay that their luggage had been stolen. The thieves had spared nothing except the couple's toilet articles and their camera case. It was assumed that the thieves didn't want the couple's personal toilet items, and authorities speculated that in their haste and loaded down with the other luggage the miscreants simply were unable to manage the camera equipment.

Well, the couple were determined not to let the incident ruin their vacation. They bought some new clothes and in fact had quite an enjoyable two weeks. They took a lot of pictures.

Upon returning home they promptly had their film developed so they could share the experience with their friends. Having shot color slides, they quickly loaded them into a Carousel projector and began showing them to their kids. Halfway through the presentation they ran across a slide they didn't take. It must, in fact, have been taken by the thieves who stole their luggage.

It was a close-up picture of the couple's toothbrushes sticking out of two large hairy butts.

• • •

Heard in Massachusetts:

I am a state trooper who works on a task force with the FBI in Boston. At work I heard that an FBI agent here was very friendly with the owner of [store name deleted], a Massachusetts clothing store chain. The clothier invited the agent on a trip to St. Maarten. On their arrival, the agent and his wife threw their suitcases on the motel bed and retreated to the pool.

When they got back to their room, it was a mess; bandits had stolen everything but their camera and their toothbrushes. Of course, their host bought his guests each a new wardrobe. They continued on their vacation, still using their camera and toothbrushes.

When they returned to Boston they had the film developed. Among their vacation pictures were two they had not taken. One was of the bandits walking out of their hotel room with the stolen suitcases on their shoulders. The other depicted a man mooning the camera. When they showed this picture to their friends, one of them noticed that the man was not simply mooning—he had both toothbrushes inserted into his anus!

I hope this isn't true.

• • •

Told in the Netherlands:

A family—father, mother, two kids—have booked a luxury bungalow in one of the Center Parcs resorts, the best-known and largest purveyor of holiday homes in the Netherlands. On the appointed day they arrive, leave their car in the parking lot, and lug their heavy suitcases to the bungalow. Much to their surprise and dismay, they discover that it is still occupied by four long-haired leather-clad bikers. They are lounging on the terrace drinking beer and smoking; their Harley-Davidsons are parked outside the holiday home.

The bikers are not in the mood to leave at such short notice. They tell the family to leave their bags and go for a stroll, which they do. For an hour or so they walk around, looking at the other guests and the shops. On their return they are very pleased to find the bikers gone. But . . . their suitcases are strangely reduced in weight. In fact, they are quite empty! How could they have been so stupid: surely they should never have left their belongings with these criminals.

But then one of the children opens a cupboard, and there is all their stuff, the clothes neatly folded and carefully stored, everything as if they had taken care of it themselves. With a sigh of relief they tell each other that, after all, appearances can be deceitful [sic]. Really nice boys those Hell's Angels turned out to be.

They have a good time in the holiday resort. Home again, they have their holiday pictures printed in the "Ready-in-an-Hour" shop. The first picture portrays four naked bottoms in a row with the family's toothbrushes stuck up their rectums.

Denver journalist and broadcaster Alan Dumas sent me the first version in March 1991; the second came from Matt Murphy of Newbury, Massachusetts, in January 1991. Peter Burger included the Dutch version in his book De gebraden baby: Sagen en geruchten uit het moderne leven *(Amsterdam, 1995). This story, titled "Vakantiefoto," is on pp. 175–76; Burger's English translation of the text collected in March 1992, was published in* FOAFtale News, *no. 30 (June 1993): pp. 5–6.*

"Gag Me with a Siphon"

Theft Attempt Left Nasty Taste

At least one potential thief in the area found out this week that siphoning gasoline out of a vehicle isn't the safest thing going.

An Iola [Kansas] area man went out Thursday morning to go to work and found a pair of brand spanking new 5-gallon gasoline cans and a hose, obviously meant to be used to siphon fuel, near his recreational vehicle.

The suspect turned out to be more of a victim than the owner of the recreational vehicle during the escapade, though.

Fumbling around anxiously in the dark, he uncapped a sewage tank rather than a fuel tank and when he put some heavy suction on the siphon tube to get things flowing, he sucked a heavy dose of the tank's contents into his mouth.

His success with the siphon tube was demonstrated by a liberal amount of vomit near the vehicle and trailing off down the road.

If there ever was poetic justice, that was it.

From Bob Johnson's "At Week's End" column in the Iola *(Kansas)* Register, *August 21, 1982.*

"Urban Pancake"

From a printout of an e-mail from the University of California, San Diego, mailed to me by "snail mail":

A friend from Berkeley just started working for the University. His supervisor had the following tale to tell.

The supervisor and his brother were going off to the 3rd game of the World Series on Oct. 17 [1989]. The brother was taking his new car, a pure white Mercedes with gold trim. He'd bought it three days before.

They get to the game, park, and go to the stands. The earthquake hits. Everyone cheers. Everyone goes out to their cars. However, our two heroes can't find their car—it's been stolen. Somehow they get home, tell the insurance company, and go on with their lives.

A couple weeks ago, the insurance company phoned back saying that they'd found the car. In fact, they'd found the thief as well—he was in the car when they found it . . . in the Cypress Structure, crushed to six inches high .

The brother was horrified, but the supervisor was really happy. "Yes, there is justice in this world!"

Many versions of this story circulated in the Bay Area following the 1989 earthquake, and this one was still going strong on the Internet some four months later. (The Cypress Structure collapsed in the earthquake.)

"Dangerous ATMs"

From an e-mail from England dated 5/1/02:

Please take note of the following advice from the police—you never know who is behind you in the queue!

The association of Chief Police Officers ATM Working Group has asked that the following information be circulated:

For your information, please be advised of the following ATM scam:

Beware the next time you use an ATM. Criminals are inventing ever more ingenious methods of relieving you of your cash.

The latest scam involves thieves putting a thin, clear, rigid plastic 'sleeve' into the ATM card slot. When you insert your card, the machine can't read the strip, so it keeps asking you to re-enter your PIN number.

Meanwhile, someone behind you watches as you tap in your number. Eventually you give up, thinking the machine has swallowed your card and you walk away. The thieves then remove the plastic sleeve complete with card, and empty your account.

The way to avoid this is to run your finger along the card slot before you put your card in. The sleeve has a couple of tiny prongs that the thieves need to get the sleeve out of the slot, and you'll be able to feel them.

• • •

From an e-mail dated 11/29/99:

URGENT!

A woman died recently from licking the deposit envelope at a BANK OF AMERICA ATM. It was laced with cyanide. Investigators stated that they went back to the ATM and found 6 other envelopes in the slot. Her death was determined by an autopsy report and of course, she became ill at the ATM. Please, implore you [*sic*] to use extreme caution when using those envelopes. The radio station advised that you should spit on the envelope and close it (I know this sounds gross, but better gross than DEAD) or keep tape in your car and tape the envelope.

PASS THIS ON AND DO TELL AS MANY AS POSSIBLE

Many descriptions of these improbable crimes circulated as e-mails, but nothing like them was ever reported in news media or by police authorities. Compare the second story to the "Icky Envelopes" stories in Chapter 9.

THOROUGHLY MODERN
HORRORS

ƒf you doubt that there are truly up-to-date horror ULs—
something more modern than ghostly hitchhikers, hook-
handed maniacs, and infested beehive hairdos—just look at
some of the topics of recent stories: AIDS, drugs, and video-
tapes, to mention only three. And, as with all contemporary
legends, these thoroughly modern horrors combine reality
with fantasy and supplement oral tradition with media circulation. Drug stories, for example, have evolved from accounts
decades ago of college women supposedly "drugged and
seduced at fraternity parties," as described in a 1973 folklore
study (Andrea Greenberg, "Drugged and Seduced: A Contemporary Legend," *New York Folklore Quarterly* 29 (1973): pp.
131–58), to detailed descriptions of the supposed horrors of
using LSD and PCP ("angel dust"), still being repeated long
after these particular drugs posed major substance-abuse
problems. Then in the 1990s, Rohypnol, the so-called date-
rape drug, accounted for some actual cases of drugged and
then raped women, as widely reported in the press.

An instance of reality being transformed by media and the
general public into legend followed the publication by the
Journal of the American Medical Association (June 3, 1988, p.

3126) of a letter from three New York doctors giving a technical, and in its own way horrible, account of a case in which a
man "administered cocaine intraurethrally prior to intercourse
to enhance sexual performance." This foolish practice, the
doctors warned, had the dire results, scientifically described in
their letter, of "extensive necrosis of skin, muscles, and subcu-
taneous tissue as well as organizing suppurative throm-
bophlebitis of popliteal and femoral arteries"; eventually the
lower part of both legs, nine fingers, and the man's penis
were lost. A number of newspapers published summarized
accounts of the letter the same year, not surprisingly focusing
on the lost members, and translating phrases like "autoampu-
tation of his necrotic penis" to simply "[his] penis fell off by
itself, doctors said." In these news stories, under a headline
such as "Cocaine User Loses Fingers, Legs, Penis," the victim
did not merely "administer" the drug, but "injected the drug
directly into his urinary tract" or "pumped cocaine into . . . his
penis." These grisly little newspaper items did not quickly
fade away; for several years following, photocopied clippings
circulated from person to person along with further sensa-
tionalized verbal accounts, some attributing the case to new
locations. Thus, the original intent of the doctors' letter—to
warn against a dangerous new form of drug abuse—was
latched onto by the press and the legend-telling public such
that the warning took on new and increasingly more dramatic forms.

Even modern institutions as prosaic as tanning salons can
inspire urban horror stories, as attested by the story in this
chapter that I call "Curses! Broiled Again!" This awful account
of a young woman who cooked her insides under tanning
lamps circulated widely for several years, always localized to
particular settings and sometimes even naming a victim
rather than using the generic "a young woman" or "a cheer-
leader from our high school." A perfectly healthy and nicely

tanned twenty-one-year-old college student in Dubuque, Iowa, even had to confront stories of her own broiling, as reported in the *Dubuque Telegraph Herald* on July 16, 1987, with the headline "Local Woman Discounts Tanning Death Rumor."

Much more serious side effects resulted from the rampant rumors of "AIDS Mary" and later "AIDS Harry." These stories tell about supposed disgruntled sufferers from this plague of our time who are determined to spread the disease via the seduction of healthy persons. The outline of these stories is always the same: an alluring stranger, a one-night stand, and a shocking note the morning after. The plot goes "I gave her love—she gave me AIDS!" as the tabloid headline put it when re-inventing the legend as a news story. Publicity about these stories inspired some hoaxes, and even some copycat sexual predators, according to news accounts.

Whatever the possible reality of these urban chillers, folkloric processes continue to operate as the rumors and stories evolve. Not only did "Mary" become "Harry," but the times and places of the encounter changed to suit the tellers and their audiences, while the manner in which the horror was unmasked ran from handwriting on the wall (in marker, pen, or lipstick) to a note left in a tiny coffin and even (in a version set on a cruise ship with a "spinster in her 40s" as the victim) to a gold-plated bracelet charm engraved "Welcome to the world of AIDS." Nobody who studies contemporary folklore would be surprised that "The Kidney Heist," an organ-theft legend, borrowed the motifs from the AIDS stories of the one-night stand and the handwriting on the wall. The latter motif occurred earlier, as we have seen, in the "Licked Hand" legend.

The "Gay Roommate" story, on the other hand, blazed a new folkloric trail by having the sedated victim of homosexual rape either trap and confront the perpetrator himself or mobilize his fraternity brothers to wreak revenge. (Be prepared to face those angry frat brothers if you point out that the "Gay Roommate" legend may symbolize latent homosexual desires on the part of the "victim," as some commentators have suggested.)

With fast-food horrors, the stories always seem to be in the realm of possibility, since we read and hear frequently about contaminated edibles, whether packaged or restaurant foods. Again, the content changes based on the locale in which a story is told; when I was in New Zealand in 1987–88 (other foreign examples follow in this chapter), I heard about a man who came into a take-out fried-chicken franchise and slung a dead possum onto the counter, saying, "That's the last one I'm going to bring you until you pay me for all the others I brought in!" This did not go over well with the other customers, since New Zealand possums (originally Australian possums) are anathema Down Under and are considered noxious pests, not dinner entrées. When I went to file that version, I found a nice item from the tabloid *Weekly World News* (September 6, 1983) that turned the American folk version of the story into a pseudo-news item under the headline "Yuk! . . . Crispy Critter in Her Lunch Wasn't Fried Chicken." To be sure that readers got the point, a photo of a whiskered, beady-eyed rat was included.

Reminding us of past supernatural legends, which underlie the tradition of modern secular legend telling, we had the short but intense career of "The Ghostly Videotape" in 1990. In this case there *was* an actual image on the taped film in question, but it was *not* what the legends claimed, certainly not a ghost. Yet—and this is the weird part—the motif of a ghost image recorded on a window or on film is an old part of folklore; how it got transferred to videotape is anyone's guess. Somehow, scary ULs easily incorporate earlier traditional themes, transforming these themes into contemporary stories.

"Drug Horror Stories"

During the 1960s groups of crazed LSD users sat and stared at the sun until they went blind.

• • •

A car full of college students was driving on a long boring stretch of freeway. The speedometer of the car was broken, and the students were smoking pot as they drove. When a state trooper pulled them over, they opened the window to fan air out of the car and ditch their stash.

Walking up to the car, the trooper asked, "Do you realize how fast you were going?"

The driver confessed that his speedometer was broken, but he didn't think he was much over the limit of 65 mph. "No," said the cop, "you weren't anywhere near 65."

The driver was surprised and asked, "Then how fast was I going, officer?"

"Eight miles an hour," the trooper replied.

• • •

Before a final exam, a worried college student studied all night, kept awake by taking No-Doz or drinking endless cups of coffee. (In other versions he took a drug to stimulate him just before the exam.) He wrote what he believed to be a brilliant essay exam.

Later the instructor called in this student to discuss the exam. It turns out that he had written all the essays on a single line of his blue book, creating just one thick black line across the page. (In another version the student merely wrote his or her name over and over again on the first page.)

• • •

Supposedly, a narc was on a bust. After successfully confiscating a large amount of sundry narcotics, the narc came across a small pill box containing a gram of a strange white substance. "Ah," said the narc, "pure uncut heroin."

In order to confirm his hypothesis, he licked the substance to check for the characteristic heroin taste. "Hm," said the narc, "this is tastless, it must be—YEOW, EIEEEEE!" He then slumped to the floor in a catatonic position.

He is now in a state institution still in his catatonic coma. For what he thought was pure heroin was actually pure acid.

• • •

Effects of PCP: Myth vs. Reality

It is a drug that has been blamed for stimulating the most abhorent mindless acts of violence.

Users are reported to have blithely amputated parts of their body—pulling their teeth out with pliers or gouging out their eyes. Mothers were accused of scalding or maiming their infants. And felons are said to have terrified police officers when gunfire failed to halt their advance or when, in a superhuman show of strength, they popped their handcuffs. . . .

It has been more than a decade since PCP—commonly known as Angel Dust and technically as phencyclidine—enjoyed its heyday. But its legacy has endured. . . .

Many law enforcement officials and prominent medical researchers and clinicians are convinced that PCP is the most dangerous drug ever to hit the streets of America.

Others are more skeptical. They say that the shocking stories about PCP are based more on myth than reality. . . .

Some medical researchers blame the media for creating a bogyman out of PCP based on a few recycled horror stories about the superhuman strength, self-destructiveness and other violence exhibited by PCP users. They acknowledge there is some truth to the stories, but stress that only a very small proportion of all PCP users suffer these extreme effects.

• • •

Popular Horror Tales of PCP Users

Horror Tales	Number of News Accounts
1. Person gouges out own eyes.	17
2. Nude, unarmed man refuses to halt on police command. Dies after varying number of police bullets are fired.	13
3. Person drowns in shower stall with four inches of water.	12
4. Young man shoots and kills own father, mother, and grandfather.	9
5. Person sits engulfed in flames, unable to perceive danger.	9
6. Person amputates a bodily part: nose, breast or penis.	9
7. Man crosses eight lane freeway, enters a house, randomly stabs pregnant woman and toddler. Toddler and fetus die; mother survives.	8
8. Pulls out own teeth with pliers.	7
9. Small 14-year-old girl requires many police to subdue her.	6
10. Seventeen-year-old runs naked through the streets in deep snow.	6
11. Motorcyclist points vehicle head-on into Trailways bus (or tree).	6
12. Person pops handcuff restraints.	5
13. Mother puts baby in cauldron of steaming water.	5
14. Person wanders onto freeway and does push-ups.	5

"Bufo Abuse"

A toxic toad gets licked, boiled, teed up, and tanned.

Plump, greenish-yellow and pebbly in texture, it is not much to look at. It can be a nuisance, too, poisoning dogs and squishing noisely under automobile tires. But *Bufo marinus*, also known as the cane toad, has become an international celebrity of late, inspiring drug-war hysteria in the U.S. and trade talks in the Far East. Here is its tale, warts and all.

This large toad—some attain the girth of Frisbees—once lived quietly in the warmer regions of the Americas, ranging as far north as central California. In the 1930s it was exported to Australia in an attempt to control beetles infesting cane fields (hence its common name). Like many amphibians, *B. marinus* wards off predators by secreting a toxic goo from glands in its skin. The secretion contains a compound called bufotenine, which resembles the neurotransmitter serotonin and also occurs in certain toadstools and plants. Although these bufotenine-containing substances can be lethal, they have reportedly been used as intoxicants by some "primitive" societies. . . .

The U.S. Drug Enforcement Administration outlawed bufotenine in the late 1960's. Ironically, the DEA's action inspired a few people to try licking live toads, says Darryl S. Inaba, director of drug programs at the Haight-Ashbury Free Medical Clinic in San Francisco, ground zero of the 1960s drug culture. But these adventurers became sick rather than high, he adds, and toad licking never caught on.

For the past two years, however, newspapers have been filled with lurid accounts of cane toad abuse. In April, 1988, *USA Today* reported that Australian "hippies" were "forsaking traditional drugs for cane toads, which they boil for a slimy, potentially lethal cocktail." Although Australian authorities have denied the story, it apparently primed the media for more. A few months later Inaba gave a lecture on drugs in which he mentioned—for comic relief, he says—the rare 1960's practice of toad licking. Soon reporters all across the world were calling to inquire about "crazed hippies licking toads in the mountains," says Alex Stalcup, director of the clinic. . . . The story persisted . . . [and] inevitably, reality imitated fiction. Last year, Stalcup says, two teenagers in New Mexico ingested cane toad toxin after reading stories about the "fad" and had to be hospitalized. An Australian youth died after eating cane toad eggs. "This rumor has caused a lot of misery," Stalcup says.

The first three items are typical drug rumors and stories found in many sources, both oral and printed. The story about the outwitted cop is from Richard M. Dorson, America in Legend *(New York: Pantheon, 1971), p. 273, as reported by a college student in 1968. "Effects of PCP . . . " is extracted from an article by Claire Spiegel in the* Los Angeles Times, *July 17, 1991. The chart of PCP horror tales is from an article by John P. Morgan, M.D., and Doreen Kagan, M.S., "The Dusting of America: The Image of Phencyclidine (PCP) in the Popular Media,"* Journal of Psychedelic Drugs *12, nos. 3–4 (July–December 1980): p. 198. "Bufo Abuse" is extracted from a report by John Horgan in* Scientific American, *August 1990, pp. 26–27.*

"Curses! Broiled Again! (and Again, and Again)"

I was looking at a newspaper ad for a tanning parlor and mentioned to one of my coworkers that I might go check it out. She got a very serious look on her face. "Oh, you better be real careful. I just heard the most awful story about those places from my cousin. Her best friend was about to get married, and she decided she wanted to have a real dark tan for the wedding. So she joined three tanning parlors and went in as often as she could, like five or six times a day. Then the day of the wedding she started feeling queasy and went to the doctor. He X-rayed her and found out that all those tanning rays had just turned her insides to mush—she had cancer all over the place and was dying. They held the wedding at the hospital, and she died just a couple of days later.

• • •

Did you hear about the poor young lady who dropped dead as a result of the injuries she received while tanning indoors? It seems the day before her wedding (or was it her prom?) a young woman decided to obtain a quick tan in order to look her prettiest for the big event. She spent the day going from salon to salon, tanning for up to an hour at each establishment. By the end of the day she had visited some-where between three and seven salons and her skin was seri-ously scorched. Her burns were so severe in fact that—you guessed it—she later died from her injuries.

Or maybe you heard the even more unlikely story about the woman who, again in an attempt to obtain a quick tan for her wedding, prom or a trip to Hawaii, spent an entire day tanning at various salons. A week or two later she started emitting a stench similar to the smell of rotten meat which no amount of soap or perfume could eliminate. In desperation, she visited her doctor who ran extensive tests and finally determined that the woman's tanning spree had somehow microwaved her insides. By the time she saw her doctor she had only a short time left to live. When the poor woman asked if there was something he could do, the doctor looked at her sadly and said, "Honey, curing this condition would be like frying a steak and then trying to bring it back to life."

. . . Unfortunately, salon owners across the country have

heard versions of such tales all too often from worried customers, concerned parents and tanning skeptics.

• • •

A: So, have you ever heard any urban legends or stories about
the tanning bed?

E: Yeah, many. OK, there was one girl—I heard this when I
was young—you know, like, when you first start getting in
the tanning bed, they tell you all this stuff—why you
shouldn't do it. There was one about this girl who was trying to go to the prom, she was going to the prom, or something like that; and she wanted to get a tan, so she kept
going to the tanning bed. And you're only allowed to get
in the tanning beds for a certain amount of time, and you
can only go at least [*sic*] one time a day, and she had, like,
two memberships at two different places, and she would
go to both ones each day. Well she did this every day, for a
while, and she got to where she didn't feel good, and she
just, one day noticed, like, in the shower, or whatever, I
don't know, but this smell, and she didn't know what it
was and so she went to the doctor because it freaked her
out really bad.

And he looked at her, and he noticed that she was
really red and really burnt, and she just, it was obvious,
you know, something was going on, so he asked her had
she been exposed, you know, to the sun or anything, and
she said, yeah she gets in the tanning bed. And then he
was like, "Well how much?" and she was like, she wanted
to lie at first, and then she told him that she wanted to be
tan really quick. And then he was like, "Well I'm sorry"
you know.

After he told her that, after, uh, she told him that, they
and he realized that, you know, she was killing herself.
And he told her that, um, she was going to die very soon—

that she baked herself to death, that it was cooking everything from the inside out—that she had just slowly, you
know, nuked her organs and everything.

A: Wow, that's—

E: And then there was this one, and I heard it a long time ago,
this is really so stupid, there was this one about this
woman who was trying to get pregnant, but she wasn't
pregnant yet, and it was summertime, and she, you know,
wanted a tan before she got this bathing suit and everything, just like most women do: that's why they go to the
tanning bed. But, um, she wanted a tan and she knew she
wasn't pregnant, and they hadn't been trying very long, so
she kept going and going, and she probably went every
day, and then she couldn't ever get pregnant, no matter
how hard they tried, you know; they'd been trying for a
short time but nothing was happening. So she went to the
doctor, and after examination, I guess, he figured out, you
know, that the tanning bed had baked her ovaries, and so
she couldn't have any kids.

The first version, partly quoted in Curses! Broiled Again!, *was sent to
me in June 1988 by Christine A. Lehman of Santa Ana, California. The
second is from an article by Linda Tien in the magazine* Tanning
Trends, *June/July 1989, pp. 30–31. The third is from Amanda Gretchen
Brown, "The Price of Skin-Deep Beauty: Some Folklore of Tanning
Salons,"* Midwestern Folklore *27 (2001): p. 16; this version was published verbatim from a recording made in November 2000 with "Erica,"
a twenty-year-old college student in Athens, Georgia.*

"AIDS Mary"

Birthday Gift Was More Than He Bargained For

Dear Ann Landers:

Several weeks ago I was told about something that happened to the son of a lovely neighbor couple. I have not been able to sleep since. Here's the story. What can I do to help?

As a birthday gift, a group of the young man's pals solicited a sexually active girl to spend three hours with him in a motel. When he was told of the "gift," he tried to get out of it, but his friends insisted that he accept it as his initiation into the "fraternity of manhood."

He met the girl in the motel room. After they had sex, she excused herself to go into the bathroom. Twenty minutes went by and she did not return, so he went to look for her. On the bathroom mirror scrawled in lipstick was the message, "Welcome to the World of AIDS."

The young man thought it was a joke. Several months later, when he was bothered by headaches, he went to see a physician. The doctor asked if there had been any changes in his behavioral pattern. He thought it best to mention the motel incident. The boy was tested for AIDS, and the results were positive.

The girl and her family have since moved out of town. That birthday was the lad's 14th. His parents are beside themselves. What can be done?

Sleepless Nights in Canada

Dear Canada:

My editor advised me not to print your letter because he said it is one of those often-repeated stories that has been around for months and may not be true. I argued that the letter should be printed (with a disclaimer) because it illustrates a crucial point: Teenagers are just as susceptible to AIDS as adults.

• • •

Never Love a Stranger

"You hear things," Natalie says. She takes a breath and leaves her bantering tone behind. "I have this friend at the office," she begins. "She told me about this friend of hers who lives in Chicago. Her friend went to a club one night and met a really attractive man and they got a little drunk and ended up going back to her place. He spent the night, but in the morning when she woke up, he wasn't there. When she went into the bathroom, she saw a message written on the mirror in her lipstick: "Welcome to the wonderful world of AIDS."

There is a silence in the little group. "I heard that story, too," Connie says. "Only I heard it happened in Boston, to a friend of my old roommate's."

It turned out, in the end, that a lot of people in the bar had heard the AIDS story. It was one of those tales that brings a shudder of vulnerability. . . .

"I guess it doesn't really matter whether it's true or not," Gwen concludes. "The problem is, it could be."

• • •

My sister-in-law's brother-in-law's friend's sister in Madison, Wisconsin, was on spring break this year in Florida. She met an older man (in his 30s) who swept her off her feet, and she extended her stay as their romance got hot and heavy.

When she left, he drove her to the airport and gave her a small box. He told her not to open the box until she was in the air. Opening the box, she found a small coffin, and inside it was a note that read "Welcome to the wonderful world of AIDS."

The girl was immediately tested for AIDS when she arrived home, and she tested positive. The police are looking for this man now—she has pictures of him—but he gave her a false name.

My husband and I find this story doubtful and wonder if this is a new urban legend for the '90s.

The Ann Landers column ran on July 30, 1987. "Never Love a Stranger" is from the "Eyewitness" column by Lynn Darling in Mademoiselle, *September 1987. Nancy Rydzak of Slingerlands, New York, sent me this "small coffin" version of "AIDS Harry" in April 1990.*

"Kidney Heists"

I heard a story last night from my best friend in Ohio who heard it from his brother—a Fairfax Co., Virginia, policeman. This happened to a friend of a friend of his:

A group of guys went to New York City for the weekend to "whoop it up." They were having a good time in a bar when one of them met a woman and they began to hit it off. He went back to the guys and said, "Listen, I'm going with this woman to her place and if I get lucky you won't see me till tomorrow afternoon, so don't worry." And they left.

Morning came and the guy who separated from his friends was not back, but no one worried till they got a phone call from him. "I think I'm at XYZ Hotel," he said, "and I think in room 223. But something's wrong with me and you have to come and get me."

The friends rushed to XYZ Hotel where they had to force the door open. They found their friend lying in a blood-soaked bed. Something was very wrong, but they saw nothing amiss until they turned him over and saw a fresh surgical closure still bleeding. He was rushed to the hospital where it was discovered that he had had a kidney removed. The guy had been drugged, his kidney removed and sold on the black market.

This must be an urban legend. Is it new? Where is it circulating? Have you heard it yet?

• • •

This came to me from my cousin in Harlingen, Texas, who heard it from a mutual friend of ours in Bermuda Dunes, California. She told me this in January this year [1994] shortly before coming to visit me in New Orleans. Our friend in California was seriously warning her to be careful on her trip.

Recently two couples from California went to New Orleans on vacation. One night they were walking back to their hotel in the French Quarter. One man was lagging behind and when they got to the hotel he was not with them. He didn't return that night, and the following day they reported his disappearance to the police.

They returned to California about two days later without any word from the missing man. The police had no clue as to his whereabouts. Several days, or a few weeks later (I don't remember which) the wife of the missing man received a phone call from him, and when she asked what all the noise in the background was, he replied that he was calling from a pay phone in New Orleans. He wanted to know why they had gone off and left him.

He said he had found himself wandering in the French Quarter a little disoriented and with a big scar on his stomach. After he returned home he went to the doctor and discovered that he had been drugged and one of his kidneys had been removed for sale to a "body parts" group.

• • •

A couple [in Ontario, Canada] decided to do some shopping at a mall across the border in the U.S. They split up and decided that they would meet in the parking lot at their car at a specified time.

When the time came, the woman sat and waited for her husband for several hours, but there was no sign of him. She finally called the police and told them that her husband was missing. The police took down the information and looked around, but told her that there was really nothing more that they could do at that time.

The woman continued to wait and finally saw a man stumble from behind the mall and collapse. She rushed over to find her husband was the man, and she struggled to get him into the car. All he said to her was to drive over the border to the closest hospital.

It turned out that the man was grabbed in the parking lot and taken to a van where surgery was performed right in the van to remove a kidney. He was then dumped in the parking lot and left for dead.

• • •

This is not a joke. . . .

This was sent to our office by one of the partners in our firm. . . .

Dear Friends:

I wish to warn you about a new crime ring that is targeting business travelers. This ring is well organized, well funded, has very skilled personnel, and is currently in most major cities and recently very active in New Orleans.

The crime begins when a business traveler goes to a lounge for a drink at the end of the work day. A person in the bar walks up as they sit alone and offers to buy them a drink. The last thing the traveler remembers until they wake up in a hotel room bath tub, their body submerged to their neck in ice, is sipping that drink. There is a note taped to the wall instructing them not to move and to call 911. A phone is on a small table next to the bathtub for them to call. The business traveler calls 911 who have become quite familiar with this crime. The business traveler is instructed by the 911 operator to very slowly and carefully reach behind them and feel if there is a tube protruding from their lower back.

The business traveler finds the tube and answers, "Yes." The 911 operator tells them to remain still, having already sent paramedics to help. The operator knows that both the business traveler's kidneys have been harvested.

This is not a scam or out of a science fiction novel, it is real. It is documented and confirmable. If you travel or someone close to you travels, please be careful.

•   •   •

THIS HAS BEEN FORWARDED A LOT OF TIMES TO MANY DIFFERENT PEOPLE, ALL OVER AUSTRALIA PLEASE CONTINUE TO FORWARD THIS TO WHOEVER YOU CAN TO RAISE AWARENESS THAT SUCH HORRIFIC AND INTOLERABLE THINGS ACTUALLY DO OCCUR IN THE WORLD IN WHICH WE LIVE YOU ARE NEVER SAFE IN SOCIETY NEVER TAKE ANYTHING FOR GRANTED.

Medical alert

Now this is weird. This is a true story, it has been confirmed, the Medical Centre phone number at the end of this story [here deleted] is real.

This guy went out on a Saturday night a few weeks ago to a party. He was having a good time and had a couple of beers and some girl seemed to like him & invited him to go to another party. He quickly agreed & decided to go along with her. She took him to a party in some apartment and they continued to drink, & even got involved with some drugs (unknown).

The next thing he knew, he woke up completely naked in a

bathtub filled with ice. He was still feeling the effects of the drugs, but looked around to see he was alone. He looked down at his chest, which had "CALL 000 or YOU'LL DIE" written on it with lipstick. He saw a phone was on a stand next to the bathtub so he picked it up & dialed. He explained to the 000 operator what the situation was & that he didn't know where he was, what he took, or why he was really calling.

She advised him to get out of the tub. He did, and he appeared normal, so she told him to check his back. He did, he found two 20cm slits on his lower back. She told him to get back into the tub immediately, and they sent a rescue team over.

Apparently, after being examined, he found out more of what had happened. His kidneys were stolen. They are worth $10,000 each in the black market. The second party was a sham, the people involved had to be at least medical students & it was not just recreational drugs he was given. Regardless, he is currently in the hospital on a life support, waiting for a spare kidney. The University of Sydney in conjunction with the Royal Prince Alfred hospital is conducting tissue research to match the victim with a donor. . . .

I REALLY WANT AS MANY PEOPLE TO SEE THIS AS POSSIBLE SO PLEASE SEND THIS TO WHO EVER YOU CAN.

Felicia S. Strobert sent me the initial version above—the very first copy that I received of this quickly spreading legend—in a letter written from her home in Stone Mountain, Georgia, dated March 8, 1991. I soon determined that this was indeed a "new" urban legend, as many more versions soon started arriving, only a very small selection of which is included here. The second version was sent by Sue Kachtik of Harahan, Louisiana, in March 1994. The third came sometime in 1993 from Gail King of Ancaster, Ontario. The first of the two e-mailed warnings is a text that was very widely forwarded almost verbatim in the following several years; this one came to me in 1997 and, like many others, was circulating on a company's computer network. I deleted the names and identifications of the supposed authenticating persons on both this one and the second e-mailed warning, which came to me from Australia in September, 2000.

"The Gay Roommate"

This guy—a friend of the narrator's cousin—goes to the University of Maryland at College Park. During the first semester of his freshman year he develops a sort of illness, a rash on the bottom being the major symptom.

After a consultation with a doctor the student is bluntly advised to "stop engaging in homosexual acts." The student, aghast at this allegation, proclaims the doctor to be a quack and testifies to his heterosexuality. Angry, he storms from the doctor's office.

The student later receives a call from the same doctor with the results of blood tests. Apparently the odd thing about this student's case is that he has an unusual amount of formaldehyde in his blood.

Determined to find out what has been going on, the guy waits up at night. Then he sees, in the darkness, his roommate get up, go to the medicine cabinet, douse a rag with a strong-smelling chemical, and move towards his bed.

Of course, the guy leaps from his bed, switches on the light, and beats the roommate to a pulp.

It turns out that the roommate had been knocking the guy unconscious with formaldehyde and sodomizing him during the night. The roommate was expelled. This story is known among my friends and me as "The Formaldehyde Man."

• • •

This story is true; I know it's true. A friend of my room-mate's—freshman year—he knew the dude, a guy on the floor of his dorm. This guy at the other end of the floor, he was kind of an alcoholic. A lot of times he'd have a few drinks, and he would black out, and he'd wake up, and he'd find that his butthole—his anus—was sore. He didn't really think too much of it; he thought it was just like a rash or something.

And it kept getting worse, and he'd notice the nights he'd drink and black out, he'd wake up and his anus was all sore. And he went to a doctor, to ask him, "Why's my butt all sore?" and the doctor said to him, "You gotta stop having anal sex so much." And he said, like, "Dude, no way; I'm not a fag or nuthin; I'm not gay," and the doctor said, "All your symptoms say you're having anal intercourse."

The guy wanted to find out what was going on. One night he went out drinking with his buddies, but he didn't really drink much at all, so he was totally conscious of what was going on. He lay down in a beanbag chair to watch TV, and he pretended to pass out, to find out what was going on.

His roommate came up, and he had a handkerchief full of ether, and he tried to knock him out. He figured out that every night his roommate was giving him ether, and he would pass out, and I guess his roommate would [sodomize him] or something. Anyway, he got some guys in his frat to beat the crap out of him. Later when he was looking through the trash, he found a bunch of bloody condoms.

Well, anyway, that's a true story, man.

The first version was sent to me by Mike Clark, then a freshman at the University of Maryland in Baltimore County, in October 1990; he wrote that he changed "a vulgar term usually used in telling it." The second version was tape-recorded by Henry Klotkowski from his roommate in

December 1992, as part of an assignment in a popular-culture class at Michigan State University; I slightly repunctuated the text and replaced one vulgar phrase with the technical term.

"Fast-Food Horrors"

"The Kentucky Fried Rat"

This was told to me by a good friend in 1969 or 1970. I was nineteen years old at the time and going to college in my hometown of Danbury, Ct. The story was told to my friend by her grandmother, who claimed it happened to a friend of a friend.

A husband and wife decided to go to a drive-in movie in Danbury, and prior to going they got a bucket of chicken at the Kentucky Fried Chicken restaurant on Route 7 on the Danbury-Brookfield Rd. At the theater they were enjoying the film and eating their chicken when the wife complained of a funny taste of the piece of chicken she was eating. The husband turned on the dome light to inspect the chicken.

At that point they realized that she had been eating a complete batter-fried rat. She screamed, and the husband had to rush her to the Danbury Hospital. She eventually had a nervous breakdown and was committed to Fairfield Hills, a mental hospital in Newtown, Ct.

"Kentucky Fried Rat in South Africa"

This happened during the 1980s, at the height of the sanctions campaign, when many companies were disinvesting in South Africa. People kept looking for clues that a company was about to pull out.

Kentucky Fried Chicken suddenly launched a new advertising campaign with new characters replacing Colonel Saunders [sic]—I think they were a wolf and a crow. So people said they were planning a name change, and were familiarising the public with their new image, as the parent company was going to disinvest.

Well, Kentucky refuted the name change claim, but they did finally announce their disinvestment. The workers at the Hillbrow branch were really furious, because they thought they were going to lose their jobs.

So they put rats in the batter. People didn't notice the difference, because it tasted just as good. But someone got sick while eating it, and took a closer look, and that's how it came out.

"Rats in the Pizza"

I heard [this] for the first time in September 1973. An eighteen-year-old girl, living in my family as a nursemaid, told it. She said that a friend of her fiancé had been eating at an Italian pizza restaurant in Stockholm together with some fellow students. One girl in the party suddenly got a sharp object stuck between her teeth which she could not take away. The next day she went to a dentist, who removed the object and established that it was a tooth from a rat. The girl reported the restaurant to the National Health Board, and an inspection was carried out. The result was that a large number of flayed, deep-frozen rats were discovered. My informant felt extremely disgusted and claimed that she would never more visit a pizza restaurant.

"Hold the Mozzarella!"

This was told to me by a coworker who swore it had actually happened to the friend of another coworker's grandmother.

A lady and her husband, both senior citizens, order pizza from Domino's. When it arrives, the woman pays for it, and she and her husband are about to sit down and eat it when the phone rings.

She picks up the phone and the voice on the other end asks, "Did you get your pizza?" When she replies, "Yes," the caller says, "Good, because I just made your pizza and I masturbated on it," and he then hangs up.

The couple takes the pizza to the hospital where it is examined and found to contain semen. The Domino's employee is arrested and sent to prison.

"Hold the Mayo!"

Here's something an ex-girlfriend once told me. We were at a Greek coffeehouse—there are hundreds of them in New York City. The food is strictly American, but the owner and waiters are usually Greek.

We'd both ordered burgers with side orders of fries. On each of our plates was a little Dixie cup filled with coleslaw. I began to dig into the coleslaw, when my girlfriend reached over to stop me. "Don't eat the coleslaw!" she said. "The cooks at these places whack off in it."

"Hold Everything!"

A friend of a friend [in Australia] went for a burger at the local takeaway. As he chomped into the salad-filled bun, he thought that it was rather chewy. Being in a hurry though, he didn't investigate. When he got near the end of the burger, he eventually dissected it and discovered a green condom hidden amongst the lettuce leaves.

The first "Kentucky Fried Rat" was sent to me by Mark A. Catone of

Danbury, Connecticut; the second is from Arthur Goldstuck's The Aardvark and the Caravan: South Africa's Greatest Urban Legends *(London: Penguin Books, 1999), pp. 143–44. "Rats in the Pizza" is the title story of Bengt af Klintberg's* Råttan I Pizzan: Folksägner I vår tid *(Stockholm: Norstedts Förlag, 1986), p. 62; I quote the English text from Klintberg's "Modern Migratory Legends in Oral Tradition and Daily Papers,"* Arv: Scandinavian Yearbook of Folklore *37 (1981): p. 154. "Hold the Mozzarella!" was sent to me by James Black of Irving, Texas, in May 1993. "Hold the Mayo!" was sent by Max Cantor of New York City in January 1988. "Hold Everything!" is from Graham Seal,* Great Australian Urban Myths, Revised Edition: The Cane Toad High *(Sydney and New York: Harper Collins, 2001), page 87.*

"The Ghostly Videotape"

A story is circulating in our area about the movie "Three Men and a Baby." Someone saw the story on the "Current Event" TV show, and another read an article on it somewhere else.

It refers to a portion of the movie about midway through, where Ted Danson's character's mother [played by Celeste Holm] comes to visit. In the background, you can see a boy, about 7–9 years old, standing in the shadows by the window curtains. His back is to the window. He is facing into the room. The look on his face is chilling.

The story we heard is that a woman who used to rent the apartment where the film was shot in New York City went to see the movie to see her old apartment. This woman had a young son who fell from a window of that apartment when she lived there. It was a fatal fall.

She went to pieces in the movie theater when she saw her son standing by the window in the background of that scene.

She supposedly contacted the producers who denied any other children were used or were on the set of the movie.

Locally, everyone who has heard this story has rented the movie. It was on our local channel last week, and it *always* shows the boy. I hope you have the resources to help explain this.

Sent to me in September 1990 by Maureen Bennett of Canastota, New York, one of dozens of similar reports I received that autumn. Some claimed the story was revealed on the TV program 20/20; others said the boy had killed himself with a rifle that was also visible in the scene. All claimed that the "ghost" was visible only on the videotape, not the theater screen. What everyone had actually seen was a cardboard stand-up cutout of actor Ted Danson slightly out of focus in the background.

CHILLER E-MAILS AND OTHER SCARY NETLORE

The very first story quoted in this book came from an e-mail, and examples of other scary ULs circulating through the electronic grapevine appeared in subsequent chapters, so it's appropriate to conclude this collection with a few additional legends captured from cyberspace. The electronic transmission of urban rumors and legends has become their chief means of circulation, supplementing the traditional sharing of such folklore via word of mouth or print. If you recognize some of the legends collected in this book, it's likely that you encountered them on the Internet, usually in the form of what I call "bogus warnings" e-mailed to you by concerned friends and acquaintances or posted to online discussion groups. Maybe you have even been guilty of passing on such stories yourself!

The Internet is a wonderful tool for rapid archiving, researching, and debunking of ULs—just look at the fine work being done at the site called www.snopes.com; then follow the links to their sources and counterparts at other URLs. But the Internet also makes it possible for bizarre, sensational, scary, and often highly doubtful stories to fly around the world with the speed of a mouse-click. In fact, the role of the

Internet in simply transmitting ULs is probably far greater at present than its success in exposing them as unreliable accounts. Even when a story is identified and revealed as a mere legend, that doesn't stop it from being forwarded and retold; after all, as I like to say, "The truth never stands in the way of a good story." Besides, the lessons a story teaches may be worthwhile, even if the story itself is apocryphal (e.g., remember to check the backseat of your car, even if the chances of a serial killer's lurking there are, at best, highly remote).

But how do you *know* that scary warnings about, say, violent gang initiations or attempted abductions e-mailed to you by your aunt Agnes are not legit? Shouldn't you pass them on (as the messages invariably request) "just in case"? Before you clutter the Internet with more copies of these alarming messages, consider this: If there were indeed such a rash of criminal assaults, dangerous acts, and unsafe products around, wouldn't we learn of them from official government channels or through the media instead of just via e-mails from friends and relatives? Also, observe the form and style of these typical warnings, noting the many times they've been forwarded already (often indicated by carets at the beginnings of lines), the generous use of ALL CAPS, exclamation points!!!!!!!!, and vague references like "Authorities have warned that . . . " Even when specifics are cited, they generally take the hazy form of something like "Three families in the Midwest have already fallen victim to this scam" or "Police report that this is happening all over." It's funny that these crimes never made the news. Of course, the best tip-off is when an e-mailed warning simply echoes the plot of an earlier urban legend, such as "The Killer in the Backseat" or "The Hairy-Armed Hitchhiker."

But people *do* believe the chilling e-mails, or at least they continue to pass them on, sometimes adding little notes of their own, such as "Be Aware!" or "Send this to everyone you know!" or even (as I saw once) "This is the absolute Internet truth!" (whatever that means).

Lou Gonzales, a writer for the *Colorado Springs Gazette*, made this astute comment in a 1999 column:

> In this high-tech world, Americans have become particularly susceptible to the "gullibility virus," a stubborn strain that weakens a person's ability to question what they read on e-mail, no matter how outrageous, and compels them to e-mail copies of dubious tales to all their friends and acquaintances.

Bogus or real (I've seldom seen a real one), these e-mailed warnings and chat-room comments can be very scary. Like many other scary urban legends, they play on people's fears of random unprovoked violence, criminal scams, and injuries from faulty products. The typical settings of the warning stories are commonplace sites, like highways, service stations, shopping malls, and fast-food restaurants. The common claims of some "new gang initiation" or "a ploy being used by many criminals" are made more believable and dramatic by relating a chilling little story about "a friend" or "a lady in California" to whom this really happened. Often the warnings conclude with a reference to a claimed source of information (like CNN, *Inside Edition*, or the Centers for Disease Control and Prevention), and sometimes they include even the name and identification, complete with telephone number, of a person who can verify the information. Usually, if you call, you learn either that the cited person does not exist or that the person was merely the latest to forward the warning.

There is less variation among versions of Internet legends than among urban legends transmitted orally, simply because most people forward the Internet stories exactly as they received them. Variations sometimes crop up when the senders add local touches or even combine versions of stories they have received. I've quoted a few examples containing such variations on a theme, but a published work can never keep up with the speed of electronic transmission. By the time you read this, there will certainly be many other frightening e-mails going around just waiting for either gullible recipients to forward them or perhaps for skeptical recipients to delete them.

"Killers in Cars"

BE AWARE—PLEASE READ

THIS IS TOO SERIOUS . . . . . DO NOT DELETE. PLEASE PASS IT ON!

A friend stopped at a pay-at-the pump gas station to get gas. Once she filled her gas tank and after paying at the pump and starting to leave, the voice of the attendant inside came over the speaker. He told her that something happened with her card and that she needed to come inside to pay. The lady was confused becaue the transaction showed complete and approved. She relayed that to him and was getting ready to leave but the attendant once again, urged her to come in to pay or there'd be trouble. She proceeded to go inside and started arguing with the attendant about his threat. He told her to calm down and listen carefully: He said that while she was on the other side pumping gas, a guy slipped into the back seat of her car on the other side and the attendant had already called the police.

She became frightened and looked out in time to see her car door open and the guy slip out. The report is that the new gang initiation thing is to bring back a woman and/or her car. One way they are doing this is crawling under girls/women's cars while they're pumping gas or at grocery stores in the night time. The other way is slipping into unattended cars and kidnapping the women. Please pass this on to other women, young and old alike. Be extra careful going to and from your car at night. If at all possible, don't go alone! This is real!!

The message:

1. ALWAYS lock your car doors, even if you're gone for just a second!
2. CHECK underneath your car when approaching it for reentry, and check in the back before getting in.
3. Always be aware of your surroundings and of other individuals in your general vicinity, particularly at night!

Send this to everyone so your friends can take precaution.
AND GUYS. . . YOU TELL ANY WOMEN YOU KNOW ABOUT THIS

Thanks,

This 2002 warning has elements of two older scary ULs, "The Killer in the Backseat" and "The Slasher under the Car" (see Chapter 2), plus the more recent addition of the crime as a "new gang initiation thing." The copy forwarded to me bore the name of a woman said to be "Secretary, Directorate of Training, U.S. Army Military Police School" and a telephone number in the 573 area code.

"Needle Attacks"

Subject: Not a Joke!!!IMPORTANT ISSUE
Date: Fri, 11 Dec 1998
PLEASE READ IMPORTANT MESSAGE BELOW AND SEND TO ANYONE I MIGHT HAVE MISSED!
A very good friend of mine is in an EMT certification course. There is something new happening that everyone should be ware of.
Drug users are now taking their used needles and putting them into the coin return slots in public telephones. People are putting their fingers in to recover coins or just to check if anyone left change, are getting stuck by these needles and infected with hepatitis, HIV, and other diseases. This message is posted to make everyone aware of this danger.
Be aware! The change isn't worth it!
P.S.—This information came straight from phone company workers, through the EMT instructor. This did NOT come from a hearsay urban legend source. [Michigan]

• • •

Subject: BE CAREFUL AND PLEASE READ!!
Date: Tue, 01 Feb 1999

I know that some of you don't like this kind of stuff but its really important, so please read!!- -kathy

READ THE FOLLOWING PLEASE
BE CAREFUL AT MOVIE THEATRE!!
This has occurred in Hawaii and California and may be catching on
A young lady went to the movies—when she sat down she felt something poking her—she stood and found a needle with a note attached reading "Welcome to the real world, you're HIV positive."

The needle was tested and contained the HIV virus.

The needle was wedged into the seat fold. Please check where you sit—not just at the movies but all other public places—and watch where you put your hands. This is becoming a sick world—be careful. [Texas]

• • •

Vi-I know you don't like to read, but read this!!! I got it from my boy Scout scoutmaster who received it from his nephew who lives in Buffalo. Says its really happening in Buffalo so I thought I would pass this on as it could occur almost anywhere. Just having gone through HIV training on Monday for the MERT team emphasizes this even more. We have some really sick people out there!

DANGEROUS PRANK:***********Please read and forward to anyone you know who drives. My name is Captain A—— S—— of the Buffalo, New York Police Department. I have been asked by state and local authorities to write this email in order to get the word out to car drivers of a very dangerous prank that is occurring in numerous states. Some person or persons have been affixing hypodermic needles to the underside of gas pump handles. These needles appear to be infected with HIV positive blood. In the Rochester area alone there have been 17 cases of people being stuck by these needles over the past five months. We have verified reports of at least 12 others in various states around the country. It is believed that these may be copycat incidents due to someone reading about the crimes or seeing them reported on the television. At this point no one has been arrested and catching the perpetrator(s) has become our top priority. Shockingly, of the 17 people who where stuck, eight have tested HIV positive and because of the nature of the disease, the others could test positive in a couple years. Evidently the consumers go to fill their car with gas, and when picking up the pump handle get stuck with the infected needle. IT IS IMPERATIVE TO CAREFULLY CHECK THE

HANDLE of the gas pump each time you use one. LOOK AT EVERY SURFACE YOUR HAND MAY TOUCH, INCLUDING UNDER THE HANDLE. If you do find a needle affixed to one, immediately contact your local police department so they can collect the evidence. ********PLEASE HELP US BY MAINTAINING A VIGILANCE AND BY FORWARDING THIS EMAIL TO ANYONE YOU KNOW WHO DRIVES. THE MORE PEOPLE WHO KNOW OF THIS THE BETTER PROTECTED WE CAN ALL BE. [New York, via Texas]

These are just samples of the huge number of needle-attack warnings that flew about via e-mail in the late 1990s. The immediate sources of these versions, as they were forwarded to me, are indicated in square brackets after each item. Several of them were specifically attributed to a spokesperson of some kind of military or law enforcement unit, but I have dropped these attributions and their contact information to protect these sources, if, indeed, they even exist.

"Perfume Attacks"

Watch out-this is for real!

I just heard on the radio about a lady that was asked to sniff a bottle of perfume that another woman was selling for $8.00 (In a mall parking lot). She told the story that it was her last bottle of perfume that sells for $49.00 but she was getting rid of it for only $8.00, sound legitimate?

That's what the victim thought, but when she awoke she found out that her car had been moved to another parking area and she was missing all her money that was in her wallet (total of $800.00). Pretty steep for a sniff of perfume!

Anyway, the perfume wasn't perfume at all, it was some kind of ether or strong substance to cause anyone who breathes the fumes to black out.

SO, Please beware . . . Christmas time is coming and we will be going to malls shopping and we will have cash on us.

Ladies, please don't be so trusting of others and beware of your surroundings-ALWAYS! Obey your instincts!

• • •

WARNING FOR THE LADIES-Warning for women (not a joke)
Would we fall for this one? I sincerely hope that our antennae would pick up the danger in this. Please be careful.....

A cousin of an EPS Staff members was approached yesterday afternoon around 3:30pm in the Fairview Mall parking lot by two males, asking what kind of perfume she was wearing. Then they asked if she'd like to sample some fabulous scent they were willing to sell her at a very reasonable rate. She probably would have agreed had she not received an email some weeks ago warning of a "Wanna smell this neat perfume?" scam. The men continued to stand between parked cars, probably waiting for someone else to hit on. She stopped a lady going towards them, pointed at them, and told her about how she was sent an e-mail at work about someone walking up to you at the malls or in parking lots, and asking you to SNIFF PERFUME that they were selling at a cheap price.

THIS IS NOT PERFUME-IT IS ETHER!
When you sniff it, you'll pass out. And they'll take your wallet, your valuables, and heaven knows what else. If it were not for this e-mail, she probably would have sniffed the "perfume."

PLEASE BE ALERT, AND AWARE!! THIS APPLIES TO MOMS, DAUGHTERS, GRANDMOTHERS, AUNTS, SISTERS, FRIENDS. IF YOU ARE A MAN AND RECEIVE THIS, PASS IT ON TO YOUR WOMEN FRIENDS AND FAMILY!

• • •

Subject: ASAP IMPORTANT!

Seven women have died after inhaling a free perfume sample that was mailed to them. The product was poisonous. If you receive free samples in the mail such as lotions, perfumes, diapers, etc.— Throw them away! The government is afraid that this might be another terrorist act. They will not announce it on the news because they do not want to create panic or give the terrorists new ideas.

Send this to all your family and friends.

PLEASE PASS ON TO ALL WOMEN YOU KNOW!

These three warnings circulated as e-mails in 1999, March 2003, and June 2003, respectively. The first is typical of the early form of the text, ending with the (probably inadvertent) pun "Obey your instincts!" In the second version, "EPS" refers to the McGill University (Montreal) Earth and Planetary Society, where this particular form of the warning circulated; in this version, earlier e-mailed warnings are credited with saving another potential victim of a perfume attack. The subject line of the third much-forwarded warning caused my spam filter to classify the message as "Junk," but I peeked anyway. This item concluded with the name of a woman in a county attorney's office in Houston, Texas.

"More Dangers at Malls"

Date: Tue, 30 Jun 1998
This is a true story. . . and certainly worth taking the time to read. . .
Pls pass on!

Just be on your P's and Q's when you are out. God only knows what type of freaks lurk in the street. God Bless us all with what

we have to deal with. Good story for women to know about-
although with the NUTS in todays world, everyone needs to be
careful (not just women).

A woman was shopping at the Tuttle Mall in Columbus. She came
out to her car and saw she had a flat. She got her jack, spare out
of the trunk. A man in a business suit came up and started to
help her. When the tire had been replaced, he asked for a ride to
his car on the opposite side of the Mall. Feeling uncomfortable
about doing this, she stalled for awhile, but he kept pressing her.
She finally asked why he was on this side of the Mall if his car
was on the other. He had been talking to friends, he claimed. Still
uncomfortable, she told him that she had just remembered
something she had forgotten to pick up at the mall and she left
him and went back inside the mall. She reported the incident to
the mall security and they went out to her car. The man was
nowhere in sight. Opening her trunk, she discovered a brief case
the man had set inside her trunk while helping her with the tire.
Inside was rope and a butcher knife! Taking the tire to be fixed,
the mechanic informed her that there was nothing wrong with
her tire, that if it had been flat, it must have just had the air let
out of it!

• • •

!!!!!! IMPORTANT PLEASE READ

Subject: IMPORTANT!!!!!!IMPORTANT PLEASE READ
Date: Tue, 11 Apr 2000

Be careful out there!!!
The notice below was posted on JCPenny's e-mail this morning
to all Female Associates. I wanted to pass the information on
to you.

Recently on Inside Edition there was an article about several new scams to abduct women. In one, a man comes up to a woman in a Mall or Shopping Center and asks if she likes pizza. When she says she does, he offers her $100,000 to shoot a commercial for Pizza, but they need to go outside where the lighting is better. When the woman goes out of the mall she is abducted and assaulted.

Another ploy is a very nicely dressed man asks a woman if she would be in a public Service announcement to discourage drug use. The man explains that they don't want professional actors or celebrities; they want the average mother to do this. Once she leaves the mall she is a victim.

The third ploy, and the most successful, a very frantic man comes running in to the mall and asks a woman to please help him, his baby is not breathing. She runs out of the mall following him and also becomes a victim. These have been happening in well-lit parking areas, in daylight as well as night time, all over the country. The abductor usually uses a van to abduct the woman.

. . . A woman was shopping at the Tuttle Mall in Columbus. She came out to her car and saw she had a flat. . . .

• • •

I want to share a TRUE story with all of you. I heard about this last week and found out, that it is indeed TRUE. This happened to C—— C——'s sister, who lives in North Guyton. She went to the Wal-Mart in Pooler about 11:00 one night about 1–2 weeks ago. (I'm sure this is familiar for a lot of us) When she parked her car, there was a van right next to her. She heard noise coming from inside but didn't see anyone in it. (didn't think much about it then) About 1 a.m. she was leaving and noticed that the van was now parked in front of her vehicle. Getting a little nervous (that gut feeling) she went back inside and asked if a security guard could walk her out. As they were loading her car, the van pulled out and left. As she got on the road, she noticed the same van behind her.

She went a little ways (between Pooler and Faulkville) and her car began to spit and sputter. By this time she was really scared and called 911 from her cell phone. As she pulled over, the police was right there, and the van went on by. While talking to the police the van had turned around and went back by. She pointed it out and the police went after it. The man inside was arrested and taken to jail, but was released on a $700 bond. In his van they found: HER gas cap, a gun, hunting knife, duct tape, rope, a gallon jug of sugar water, and two pairs of women's underwear!!!!!!!!!

After getting her vehicle checked out for the problem, it was determined that sugar and water had been poured into her gas tank. They have found the man and he is back in jail. He is from Walterboro, S.C. I thought I would share this with you since Christmas shopping nights are just ahead. PLEASE be aware of your surroundings where ever you go. As for me, I'm getting a LOCKING gas cap. They sell them (where else but) Wal-Mart. Anyway, the bottom line is: BE CAREFUL !!!!!!!!!!!!!

"I don't know what tomorrow may hold, but I do know who holds tomorrow."

These updatings of "The Hairy-Armed Hitchhiker" (see Chapter 2) circulated widely as e-mails, often with personalized warnings added at the beginnings and ends by concerned citizens. The second example included the entire "Tuttle Mall" story exactly as given in the first example, but I omitted the bulk of that part of the message here. The third story incorporates very specific local details.

"Icky Envelopes"

Subject: If you lick your envelopes, you won't anymore
Date: Thu, 30 Nov 2000

In California, a lady licked the envelopes and postage stamps instead of using a sponge. That very day the lady cut her tongue on the envelope. A week later, she noticed an abnormal swelling of her tongue. She went to the doctor, and they found nothing wrong.

Her tongue was not sore or anything.

A couple of days later, her tongue started to swell more, and it began to get really sore, so sore, that she could not eat. She went back to the hospital, and demanded something be done. The doctor took an x-ray of her tongue and noticed a lump. He prepared her for minor surgery. When the doctor cut her tongue open, a live roach crawled out. There were roach eggs on the seal of the envelope. The egg was able to hatch inside of her tongue, because of her saliva. It was warm and moist. . .

This is a true story reported on CNN...

[One forwarder added: Hey, I used to work in an envelope factory. You wouldn't believe the.....things that float around in those gum applicator trays. I haven't licked an envelope for years.]

This close relative to "The Spider Bite" (see Chapter 4, and also see the introduction to that chapter for another e-mailed "Icky Envelope" warning), circulating recently on the Internet, is based on the idea of contaminated gummed paper products, which has been around since the introduction of the first gummed postage stamps in the mid-nineteenth century.

"Mutant Chickens"

KFC has been a part of our American traditions for many years. Many people, day in and day out, eat at KFC religiously. Do they really know what they are eating?

During a recent study of KFC done at the University of New Hampshire, they found some very upsetting facts. First of all, has anybody noticed that just recently the company has changed their name? Kentucky Fried chicken has become KFC. Does anybody know why? We thought the real reason was because of the "FRIED" food issue. It's not. The reason why they call it KFC is because they can not use the word chicken anymore. Why? KFC does not use real chickens. They actually use genetically manipulated organisms.

These so called "chickens" are kept alive by tubes inserted into their bodies to pump blood and nutrients throughout their structure. They have no beaks, no feathers, and no feet. Their bone structure is dramatically shrunk to get more meat out of them. This is great for KFC because they do not have to pay so much for their production costs. There is no more plucking of the feathers or the removal of the beaks and feet.

The government has told them to change all of their menus so they do not say chicken anywhere. If you look closely you will notice this. Listen to their commercials, I guarantee you will not see or hear the word chicken. I find this matter to be very disturbing. I hope people will start to realize this and let other people know.

Please forward this message to as many people as you can. Together we make KFC start using real chicken again.

Posted to an Internet discussion group in December 1999 and widely circulated in e-mails. A strong denial, titled "No Colonel of Truth," purportedly from the KFC company itself, also circulated on the Internet. A Web site of the University of New Hampshire denied that any such research had been done there.

"Spunkball"

Subject: SPUNKBALL WARNING
Date: Tue, 11 Apr 2000

We recently received this notice concerning a dangerous game that is being reported in various parts of the country and wanted to pass it along. Please keep all windows rolled up when stopped at traffic lights, or opened only slightly, as only cars with windows down are being targeted.

Groups of teenagers have been caught, in alarming numbers, playing a new and dangerous game called Spunkball. Spunkball consists of a group of teens in a car pulling up to a stop light, and looking around for a car stopped near by with an open window. When one is spotted, the teens shout, "Spunkball", and throw a gasoline soaked rag that has been wrapped in aluminum foil threw the open window. On the outside of the foil is attached a small firecracker, with the fuse lit. When the firecracker explodes, it shreds the foil, and the rag is ignited, causing a large flame that may catch the interior of the car on fire.

Spunkball playing has already claimed two lives, caused uncountable injuries due to burns, and caused thousands of dollars in damage to automobiles. The best defense, say authorities, is to keep all windows rolled up when stopped at traffic lights, as only cars with windows down are being targeted.

If you are at a red light and hear a shout of "Spunkball", and notice something come flying in your window, the best thing to do is to have all passengers immediately exit the vehicle. DO NOT try to retrieve the object, as it will ignite once the firecracker explodes.

PLEASE PASS THIS ON TO EVERYONE YOU CARE ABOUT

Although gangs are not mentioned here, this warning, which was still circulating in 2002, resembles the "Lights Out!" bogus warning of another sort of automotive assault quoted in Chapter 7.

"Saved by a Cell Phone"

Subject: Cell Phone #77

Date: Thu, 23 Jan 2003

FOR ALL WITH CELL PHONES

I never even knew about this #77 feature! This actually happened to someone's daughter. Lauren was 19 yrs old and in college. This story takes place over the Christmas/New Year's holiday break. It was the Saturday before New Year's and it was about 1 PM in the afternoon, and Lauren was driving to visit a friend.

An UNMARKED police car pulled up behind her and put his lights on. Lauren's parents have 4 children (high school and college age) and have always told them never to pull over for an unmarked car on the side of the road, but rather wait until they get to a gas station, etc. So Lauren had actually listened to her parents advice, and promptly called #77 on her cell phone to tell the police dispatcher that she would not pull over right away. She proceeded to tell the dispatcher that there was an unmarked police car with a flashing red light on his rooftop behind her.

The dispatcher checked to see if there was a police car where she was and there wasn't and he told her to keep driving, remain calm and that he had back-up already on the way. Ten minutes later 4 cop cars surrounded her and the unmarked car behind her. One policeman went to her side and the others surrounded the car behind. They pulled the guy from the car and tackled him to the ground..........the man was a convicted rapist and wanted for other crimes.

I never knew that bit of advice, but especially for a woman alone in a car, you should not pull over for an unmarked car. Apparently police have to respect your right to keep going to a "safe" place. You obviously need to make some signals that you aknowledge them (i.e. put on your hazard lights) or call #77 like Lauren did.

Too bad the cell phone companies don't give you this little bit of wonderful information. So now it's your turn to let your friends know about #77. This is good information that I did not know!!!!!!!!!!!!!!!!Please pass on to any females that you know.

Other versions of this warning that started showing up only in 2003 identified the clever female driver as "Laura" and specified which highway she was driving on and which city she was near, although these locales, of course, varied as well.

"A Cry for Help"

Subject: Don't open the door!

Date: Wed Feb 12, 2003

A Houston lady just told me that her friend heard a crying baby on her porch night before last and she called the police b/c it was late and she thought it was weird. The police told her "whatever you do, do NOT open the door." The lady then said that the baby cries were near her window and she was worried that it would crawl.to the street and get run over.

The police said, "we already have a unit on the way, whatever you do, DO NOT open the door." he told her that they think a serial killer possibly could have a baby's cry recorded and could use it to coax women out of their homes thinking that someone dropped off a baby. He said they have not verified it but have had several calls by women saying that they hear baby's cries outside of their doors when they're home alone at night. New tricks are being used to lure you to open the door!

Please pass this on! and do not open the door if you hear a crying baby.

Just call the police—911!

This warning had been addressed to fourteen recipients, mostly women, one of whom sent it to me with a skeptical note. It concluded with the name of a woman with the title "Certified Transportation Broker" and an 800 telephone number. I tried the number, which turned out to be nonoperative.